Tools to Ready the Journey

A Father's Guide to a Faith-Filled Family

Tools to Ready the Journey

A Father's Guide to a Faith-Filled Family

Ray Haywood

TRJ - Publishing

Harrisburg, North Carolina

TRJ Father's Guide Connections

Website: TRJFathersguide.com

Facebook: TRJ Fathers Guide

Email: TRJFathersGuide@Gmail.com

Twitter: @TRJFathersGuide

Instagram: trjfathersguide

Cover design by Jason Tako
Interior artwork by Jeanie Egolf

Edited by Kathryn P. McDermott
Copy Edited by Virginia Lieto

Scripture verses taken from The Holy Bible Douay-Rheims Version. With revisions and footnotes (in the text in italics) by Bishop Richard Challoner, 1749-52. Taken from a hardcopy of the 1899 Edition by the John Murphy Company. IMPRIMATUR: James Cardinal Gibbons, Archbishop of Baltimore, September 1, 1899. http://drbo.org/.

ISBN:
9781733595728 (Hard Cover)
9781733595704 (Paper Back)
9781733595711 (E-Pub)

Acknowledgments

To my loving wife Natalie, it is a great realization to know and share with you, and only you, that through our intentional parenting, we now get to look back at the family we led and built together, with a peace of mind that could only be achieved through living a life of faith. Through faith, we led our family to share in God's grace, which cascaded into the peaceful lives that our sons now share with us! A shared and realized love like no other, a reflection of our unconditional love told through our love story, living on and being handed on in love… God bless and guide our faith-filled family!

Iron sharpens iron…

A special thanks to our oldest son, Nicholas, for his writing contributions within, and who, over the years, challenged our family to step closer to our faith, which I am certain now was in preparation for sharing in this blessing! You are loved!!!

To my sons, nephews, and all the young men in my life whose journeys weighed heavily on my soul – you inspired my initial plea in prayer to strengthen our family's faith. This blessing is shared and handed on in love with you in mind!

A special thanks and appreciation goes out to Katie McDermott, my editor, whose selfless commitment to the family added to and shared so much perspective in this journey to bring you, the reader, this blessing fulfilled! To all the women and moms who will share in this blessing, it is Katie who had you in mind throughout her editing, so, enjoy. I assure you that Katie has truly taken her rightful place as the heart of this blessing shared, and for this, I am forever thankful! My thanks to Virginia Lieto, my copy editor, who conveyed clear perspective, throughout, tying the message together.

Dedicated to:

St. Joseph

The first paternal father, through the union of marriage, in the Universal Church.

Through St. Joseph accepting and taking his place in the Holy Family, the New Covenant and the sacraments were revealed to us as truth and handed down to us as a

precious gift from his foster son Jesus Christ for all followers of Christ to share in as our eternal and everlasting foundation of faith.

St. Joseph, pray for us, that we follow your example, seek out truth, and take our rightful place in the families we lead as we, too, selflessly choose to hand on the precious gifts of the New Covenant that we all share.

Table of Contents

Introduction

Shared within the pages of this book is much more than a point of view. This book outlines competencies and provides fundamental tools, which when compiled will paint a clearer picture of a father's place within a faith-filled family. Its purpose is to give perspective to the importance of the New Covenant and the sacraments within our Catholic (Universal) Church, to show how to be intentional in our thoughts and actions throughout our daily lives, and to understand the tremendous role we fathers play in the lives we nurture and form within our families.

Before we can lead, we must first follow. It is in following the example of those who came before us, and in sharing the truth seen clearly through God's grace, that we first find our place within our own faith journey and within our families. To fill that selfless, compassionate role of a father, we must first understand what it means to be a man and how to achieve that individually owned competency in our lives. Once we fully understand our own journey, then we can pass on, with intent, a clear understanding of a father's gifts within a faith-filled family.

A study guide is provided at the end of each chapter, along with note pages, to inspire individual reflection as well as small group discussion. This study guide is meant for use primarily within a men's group, and is encouraged as such, because the benefit of sharing and learning from other men's spiritual journeys promotes growth and perspective for all involved.

My sincere hope is that this book offers all who read it the opportunity to live their own lives with clarity and focus, using the competencies and tools shared. This book is intended to encourage and strengthen faith-filled families, by calling to action those intentional selfless fathers and grandfathers who already understand the importance of the competencies shared in this book. My hope is that these selfless men commit to handing on their faith-filled gifts. I pray that they freely share their own wisdom gained from important life lessons with the young men and new fathers in their congregations and communities. I also call to action all priests, pastors, deacons, and other clergy to encourage, engage in, and organize men's groups to meet in their parishes. I plead for them to make time to intentionally reach into the lives of the men in their congregations. We can all learn and grow from each other and from the satisfaction that giving returns.

With the right tools and competencies, we can all make a difference. We can reflect the light of Christ in our parishes, in our communities, and most of all, in the families we are held accountable by God to lead and nurture in the faith. If we accept and take ownership of these tools, handed on to us by others in a spirit of humility, then we can selflessly lead our families to the eternal happiness that only a life shared in God's grace can provide.

Seek out truth for yourself. Take time to gain knowledge and understanding of the New Covenant and the sacraments as they were intended for us all by our loving Father. Become competent to the meaning of the universal church and all that it makes clear and holds true. We are all God's children. We are all on this journey together. Spiritual and biological fathers, alike, need to become selfless, intentional, and diligent in reflecting moral values on our families and society. Lean into the Gospels and take your rightful seat at the table of God.

Chapter 1
The Masculine Journey

Before we can lead, we must first follow…

Our lives, as husbands and fathers, are much more than financial providers. The role of husband and father within the family is a crucial one – one that at this moment in time is not reflected clearly in the eyes of a young man coming into this role. As husbands and fathers, we are held accountable by God to not only lead our families, but also to nurture them within a moral posture that only a father who understands both free will and humility can achieve. The reality is that the decisions we make as husbands and fathers will lead our families to either living "in and of this world," or living "in a foundation of faith," which will cascade into the generations to come.

Therefore, we must be aware of our God-given place in the family and be competent and intentional in the way we carry out our responsibilities as husbands and fathers. Being competent means being properly equipped and ready to do the work at hand, which is formed when we are intentional in our day-to-day lives. Being intentional means being deliberate in our thoughts, words, and actions as we lead our families in building a solid foundation of faith in which our loved ones can grow. If we choose to lead intentionally through composure and humility, then our families will continually thrive as constant witnesses to our intentional strength and moral posture. Learning how to be competent and intentional, as leaders of our families, is a journey, the journey of a lifetime - the masculine journey.

I first explored the idea of the masculine journey in my early 40s in a men's group that I still attend today. We read a book about the masculine journey titled, *"Fathered by God"* by John Eldredge[1]. I recall wishing that I could have been handed this book when I turned 18, or when I was first married. It is the kind of book that paints clearly the parts of our life's canvas that can only be drawn through wisdom and experience. It shares competencies that not only prepare us for the journey ahead, but with the gained knowledge, future events will also take on different meanings and have better results for the intentional reader as he lives through them.

What we explored was the concept of a man's life broken down into six identifiable stages: childhood, adolescence, young adult, adult, middle aged followed by senior, or as by drawing on Eldredge's insight, we will refer to them as exploration, self-identity, self-worth, awakening, head of household, and elder. Notably, I see there is no exact age to pinpoint each stage, and some stages may even overlap in various ways with the understanding that our journeys are unique, just as we all are unique. Hopefully, you will use this information as both a challenge and a tool to grasp and grow in the humility and composure needed to successfully lead one's family in and through the masculine journey. Let's begin.

Childhood – Exploration Stage

The first stage, Childhood/Exploration, is where a boy grows and thrives and develops a passion for adventure and challenge. He has a natural will to explore and to push and test his own limits. One might think the natural activities of this stage are climbing trees, playing with toy guns and other weapons created by his own hands as well as challenging siblings and friends through dares and competitions.

As fathers, it is important to lead our sons competently and intentionally through this early stage of childhood/exploration wonder and discovery. Too often we see fathers falling short in their role by allowing mobile devices, video games, and social trends to shape their sons' notions of what childhood should be.

Generations of young men and fathers, who do not understand their own place in the world, refrain from leading their families. From this lack of fatherly leadership, the heart of the boy is pushed down in this crucial stage of development. Boys (and girls alike) can then become sheltered within the walls of their own minds, lured by situational or false truths shared through an unfiltered elite media and the so-called cultural norms that the unintentional father fails to recognize.

As fathers, we should encourage the exploration stage and lovingly share the responsibilities associated with this important stage of life with our wives, so that they, too, can understand and offer the encouragement needed. Allowing "boys to be boys" in the truest sense means allowing them to explore the world and challenge themselves, motivated by an intentional, loving, and nurturing father. The Exploration Stage is where a boy develops his passion and zeal for life ahead.

Adolescence – Self-Identity Stage

The second stage, Self-Identity/Adolescence, is where a young man questions himself: "Do I have what it takes?" He feels compelled to push away from the family and prove himself in the world.

This is normal human behavior. We become competent beings through trial and error. Mastering a sense of our own identity is a difficult process. It involves developing an understanding of our true gifts and capabilities. This needs to be recognized by the father so that he can effectively manage the emotional behaviors associated with this stage within the family dynamic. Adolescent "moments" – often manifested as rebellious streaks – can make or break families if not handled correctly. They can leave invisible scars that may damage a young man's (and the entire family's) future.

This stage can challenge the will and composure of the father, who is still facing his own challenges on the masculine journey. Fathers who are competent and intentional will not be able to stop these defiant moments from happening. This is all part of the masculine journey. But by sharing these facts with the son, a father can shed light on the events as they unfold, while subconsciously preparing his son for future challenges and how to approach them. This all poses a true test to the will of the father who, through steady composure, does not fall short while facing the potential dangers these moments might bring to his son and family. Compassion and selflessness are tools that will guide a father well through the Adolescence – Self-Identity Stage.

Young Adult – Self-Worth Stage

The third stage, Young Adult/Self-Worth, is where a young man finds deep within himself what he feels is worth fighting for – whether it be the Church, his country, a marriage, or a friendship. This stage can be confusing, or even lost to many young men, if their hearts were pushed down in the Childhood/Exploration Stage.

A lot is at stake in the development of a boy. If he is broken and loses his will early on, then all the stages of the masculine journey will be severely compromised, or even lost entirely, for him. This becomes clear at the Self-Worth Stage. The decision to commit to a cause and fight for it requires not only passion and zeal, but also a clear moral compass.

Society's influence often misdirects many of our young adult men to stand behind immoral causes (or false/situational truths) that are somehow made justified within our Godless society. Young men who are misdirected in this way exercise their free will by making choices that lead them down the road of destroying the family, an important institution God designed for our well-being and for the health of society at large. On the other hand, young men who are influenced by intentional fathers, who instill in them a firm moral posture, exercise their free will by making choices that allow them to fight the good fight while sharing in God's grace. These young men will take their rightful place in strengthening their family's foundation of faith and will ultimately build up society.

The realization that it is easier to build up a boy than to repair a man comes with a heavy weight. The needs of the family must always be recognized by fathers as their priority. Selflessness and compassion are essential tools for fathers who recognize this reality and commit to building a strong foundation of faith within their families. Sons, who experience such fathers, enter the Self-Worth Stage with a clear understanding of what is true and real, what causes are worth fighting for, and how to shield themselves from the attacks of a Godless society.

Adult – Awakening Stage

The fourth stage, Adult/Awakening, is where past experiences take on greater meaning than when we first experienced them. Things we once took for granted, we no longer take for granted. For a faith-filled man this is where God's gifts are seen in a different, more meaningful light. What was once just a family photograph on a shelf, now becomes a cherished notion of warmth and unconditional love.

What was once a house of planks and nails, now becomes a treasured home that shelters the family and provides a sacred space for gathering and sharing.

Perhaps more than any other stage, this stage can be tragically lost to the broken man. The awakening stage can take on a perverted meaning for a misdirected man who sees people and events as nothing more than objects to feed his selfish passions. Lust, greed, and addiction can quickly fill the hollows of the heart, abandoned to gross neglect within the prior stages.

It is through the efforts of a competent, intentional father that a boy can be set squarely on a true and faith-filled course throughout his own masculine journey. Nurturing of the mind, body, and, most importantly, soul is needed to become a truly humbled man.

Mid Life – Head of Household Stage

The fifth stage, Mid Life/Head of Household, is where a man becomes the leader of his family. This is the most influential stage in the masculine journey for both the father/husband and the family he nurtures. He is accountable for the health and direction of his family.

This responsibility needs to be carried out both competently and intentionally in the heart of the father/husband. The leader role is not meant to be looked upon crudely as the person in power or the one who sets the rules. How well this responsibility is executed is determined more by the family's point of view. A selfless father/husband does not need to hold authority over his family or pound his fist. His place is achieved almost silently, and subconsciously, through a series of past actions that over time, establish his place of honor and respect in the family.

The family members, themselves, may not even recognize this process as it unfolds. An inherent respect for the head of the family is the natural outcome of the selfless father/husband who nurtures and perpetuates a strong, faith-filled foundation throughout his family's life.

A father/husband in this context shields his family members from many of the outside false influences that could jeopardize and misdirect them. He does everything in his power to ensure their well being in this world and, most importantly, to prepare his loved ones for the world to come.

Senior – Elder Stage

The sixth stage, Senior/Elder, occurs toward the end of the masculine journey when the family members that the father nurtured are grown and beginning to start families of their own. In some cultures, family decisions are not made without consulting the elders. Their wisdom is highly regarded as they hold a place of honor within their families.

Sadly, this is not the case in all cultures, especially our own. We tend to place our elders on a metaphorical shelf – out of the way and out of our view. A disordered desire to feed our egos and selfish passions cause us to reject the elder's advice and influence.

As elders we should not accept careless cultural rejections but should make ourselves available to our families' needs as they arise. Our approach must be carefully measured. We must respect our adult son's role as head of household. But we must also be ready to step in when the family's well-being is in jeopardy, despite a son's best efforts (or lack thereof). The way in which we deliver our message will determine the way it will be received. As in all the stages, life reflects us.

If we are intentional heads of our household in life, then we contribute to building up families and societies that value the wisdom of seniors and honor the elder's place in the family. If we forfeit our roles as father/husband/head of household, then we help create an environment where elders are scorned and rejected within the family that God gave us.

For those of us who pass judgment that honor and respect for authority are absent from our society, as is spirituality, we must recognize how the situation might have been different if past generations of men had lived their lives as more intentional fathers and elders. We need to consciously accept our past actions and learn from our past behaviors and truly recognize the importance of selflessly handing on all the stages of the masculine journey. If we choose to move forward with intention and competence in a posture of humility and composure, then we can rise above the worldly challenges we must face and take our rightful place within our own masculine journey. The benefit to ourselves and our families will cascade through the generations as true peace of mind.

Every decision matters. Every action counts with rippling effects in the lives of our loved ones. Living in and of this world might seem like "no big deal" at the time, but the consequences of that choice, over time, will reflect poorly on our family life. What we accept as the norm is what becomes the norm for our family. We all fall short within our humanity from time to time. Our sinful nature causes us to fall short; it is not meant to be a state of mind.

Challenge yourself to take your rightful place within your family and your own masculine journey! Acknowledge the importance of following the honorable men in your life who can help ease the transition and define the thresholds as you strive to move from one stage of your journey to the next. The point is that in every stage of the masculine journey we must be willing to humbly follow before we can intentionally lead.

None of us is alone in his journey. We all have someone to turn to for the guidance we undeniably seek. Our Heavenly Father is always there for us. We should always turn to Him, especially in our moments of need.

Chapter 1 Study Guide
The Masculine Journey

Within chapter one we gain an understanding of the masculine journey and the various stages of a man's life. Let's consider how these concepts relate to our own lives.

Childhood – Exploration Stage

- How did I experience the childhood stage in my life?

- How did my father (or other father figures) encourage or discourage me in this stage?

- How did I identify with the head of household and elders of my boyhood journey?

- What were the competencies that I observed?

- How can I challenge myself to learn and grow from my childhood experiences?

Adolescence – Self-Identity Stage

- How did I push away from my own family in this stage?

- Was my father a competent head of household when I was in my adolescent stage? Explain.

- How did my defiance, and my father's response to it, affect my family at that time? Is it still affecting my family today? If so, how?

- Do I take the time needed to recall this stage in my own life to relate more compassionately to the lives of the adolescents I nurture? Explain.

- How can I develop within myself, the composure and selflessness needed to nurture the adolescents in my family today?

Young Adult – Self-Worth Stage

- Can I still identify with what I fought for when I first entered the young adult stage?

- Did I miss out on the healthy growth this stage can offer due to an unintentional head of household?

- What examples of competent, intentional heads of household did I experience during my young adult stage?

- How can I model these selfless examples to nurture the young adult men in my life today?

- What causes do I fight for today? How do I know they are morally sound?

Adult – Awakening Stage

- Can I recall when I first experienced the Awakening Stage in my masculine journey?

- Have I distorted the true meaning of this stage through vice or by following poor examples?

- Have I tried to rationalize my own vices or so-called cultural norms as "no big deal"? Why?

- How does the will of a healthy adult serve the challenges associated with the Awakening Stage?

- What is the difference between selfishness and accountability?

Mid Life – Head of Household Stage

- Who are the influential heads of household in my life and how have they interacted with my family?

- What are the competencies displayed by a healthy, intentional head of household?

- What damages have I observed from fathers/husbands who forfeited their roles as head of household/family leader within their families?

- How can I improve my capacity to be a competent, intentional head of household/family leader in my own family? Can I challenge myself to forgive and let go of past failures to grow as a father/husband and build a strong foundation for a faith-filled family?

- To whom can I reach out to if I struggle in my role of head of household?

Senior - Elder Stage

- How does the Elder Stage contribute to a family's growth? How have I assumed (or hope to assume) this role within my own family?

- Who are the Elders in my family's life, and how do I and my family interact with them?

- Why has this stage lost recognition and value in our culture? What are some possible ways to change this view within society?

- How do strong heads of households become strong Elders who hold an honored place in the family? What does it mean to be "strong" in this context?

- What is the dynamic interplay among all the stages of the masculine journey?

At this point in exploring the concept of the masculine journey, we should be aware of its value and importance within our own lives and the lives of our loved ones. We should challenge ourselves to hold each other accountable to the value that can be gained within our families from adapting these ideas into our daily lives, as we continually chip away at becoming more intentional. It takes humility, composure, and selflessness to nurture a growing family in love. The realization that we need to constantly work on ourselves, and to understand and accept our role in our own masculine journey within our families, is a daily challenge that needs to be met head on. We are human. We fall short. This is a reality that we need to accept and grow from. Humility is a learned virtue. Saying we are sorry when we fall short is a humble gesture that can bear good fruit for all involved. To build up our own families, we must first recognize the value in our lessons learned. We can now take a closer look at them rather than merely storing good or bad memories about our own fathers. Lessons become competencies, humbly accepted within an awakened heart. I once heard it said that the tragedy in a man's life is what dies inside him while he is still alive. How many men in your life does this statement ring true about? Does it ring true about you?

Notes:

_____

_____

_____

_____

_____

_____

_____

_____

_____

_____

_____

_____

_____

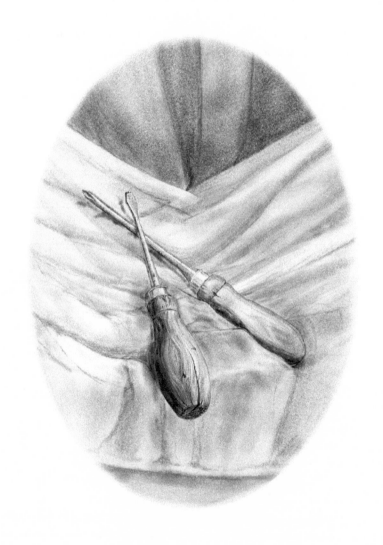

Chapter 2
Our Thoughts Are Not Our Own

You and I need to constantly be aware that we are at the center
of an epic battle… There is no neutral ground in the universe;
every square inch, every split second is claimed by God and
counterclaimed by Satan.

~ *C.S. Lewis*[2]

In this chapter we will explore the reality that our thoughts may not be of our own free will. If we believe in God, then we must believe in the devil as well. The sad reality is that the world we all now live in, conditions us not to think of either with intent. Most people live in and of this world. They find instant gratification in what their physical senses tell them and take no notice of the spiritual elements that constantly surround and stir them.

Society has conditioned us to view people who hold deeply spiritual beliefs as weak or irrational. This notion is built on the argument that if so many religions exist in the world, then how can any one of them be true? This reality lies deep in our subconscious, used as a tool, or even worse, as a weapon to confuse and separate us from objective truth. Society now holds up as the true intellectuals those who are smarter than any intolerant religion; those who rise above the superstitious notions of the simple-minded. Could this be intentional? How did this point of view become our new norm? Is it possible that we have been conditioned to think this way from generations of manipulation?

Free will allows us to choose our own direction in our physical life. Our free will allows us to choose (or reject) a relationship with God in our spiritual life. We must be aware that we have this freedom to choose. We must also be aware that the enemy, the devil, knows this fact all too well.

Satan knows it is easier to tempt vice than to embrace virtue. As humans, created in the image and likeness of God, we have an innate sense of right and wrong; as sinners, we are inclined to submit to vice. Satan seeks to encourage that inclination. He comes along, always at the most opportune time, and whispers in our ear that we are not good enough, that we are failures, that we have no willpower. This cycle repeats until we feel utterly worthless – or, alternatively, until we become so puffed up with false pride that we cannot recognize our true self. We submit to moral relativism where our new norm mirrors the worldly acceptance of a sinful mindset that results in no consequence. This worldly mindset keeps poor souls from understanding and embracing objective truth. As this subjective truth sinks in can we still accept and come to understand the consciousness of a sinful mindset? Do we acknowledge that many have lost sight of what falling into sin, and repentance through contrition means? Because of moral relativism, our innate sense of right and wrong is no longer easy to decipher. When we look at our peers, we compare our situation to theirs and perceive that "the grass is greener" over there. We begin to test the limits and embrace what the world tells us is good. Vice gets cast in a virtuous hue, and we imitate the behaviors embraced by those we perceive to be the smarter, happier people.

After generations of this morally relativistic behavior, we have almost completely removed God from our society. Was this all of our own free will? Have we been duped? As smart people, our societal perception is that we no longer require the crutch of God or religion. We use our free will to determine for ourselves what is true in this finite world. We choose to become the gods of our own physical universe. We choose to define our own system of right and wrong and have learned how to rationalize this in our accepted sinful mindset. Yes, Satan has succeeded at chipping away at our moral fiber in this world to the point where there is little work left for him to do to own our souls for eternity.

To serve as an example of how moral relativism eats at the soul, I call on C.S. Lewis's passage in the *Screwtape Letters*.[3] To set the stage, the senior demon Screwtape explains to his novice demon nephew, Wormwood, yet another tool to illustrate how to steal a man's eternal soul. In this letter, Screwtape refers to "the Enemy," meaning God, the source of all truth, goodness, and beauty. Screwtape reveals that his preferred weapons of mass destruction against man, whom he calls the "patient," are fear, vice, and pride.

My dear Wormwood,

Think of your man as a series of concentric circles, his will being the innermost, his intellect coming next, and finally his fantasy. You can hardly hope, at once, to exclude from all the circles everything that smells like the Enemy: but you must keep shoving all the virtues outward till they are finally located in the circle of fantasy, and all the desirable qualities inward into the Will. It is only in so far as they reach the Will and are there embodied in habits that the virtues are really fatal to us. (I don't, of course, mean what the patient mistakes for his Will, the conscious fume and fret of resolutions and clenched teeth, but the real center, what the Enemy calls the Heart.) All sorts of virtues painted in the fantasy or approved by the intellect or even, in some measure, loved and admired, will not keep a man from Our Father's house: indeed, they may make him more amusing when he gets there.

Your affectionate uncle,
SCREWTAPE

Take a moment to picture the three circles in your head and lock in that vision. Now let's consider applying this concept as we identify and disregard all the information we process in our lives as we discern identifying objective truth.

The first and innermost circle, our will, is our heart, whatever settles here is our foundation. Our foundation, or innermost circle, is impenetrable if it is formed with virtue that leads us to God. The second circle is our intellect, or reasoning, which can be swayed if the innermost circle is not yet fully shaped and guided by decisions made in moral posture. The third circle, fantasy, is where our free will is most easily compromised, where thoughts of truth and honor are challenged easily.

Living in and of this world leads us to question God. The prevailing cultural belief that we are smarter than the Truth becomes the accepted morality of those who have permitted their free will to operate predominantly within the realm of fantasy. Within this posturing, we lack the humility to acknowledge God as the source of all truth, goodness, and beauty. We become incapable, therefore, of discerning what is real or virtuous, as our cultural norms become more and more palatable with each new generation.

Without faith in God, and the realization of His truth, no other truth can be reasoned. For the faithful, seeing truth in this world is easy. The faithful direct their intellect and reasoning toward truth, which leads to clarity and virtue, which settle firmly within their will (or heart). This strong foundation – this true will – enables the faithful to live through life's challenges with a clear perspective of the eternal truth, which is not a concept but our loving Father. In the light of Truth, everything is seen with clear eyes.

Chapter 2 Study Guide
Our Thoughts are Not Our Own

In chapter two, we considered the question of whether our thoughts are truly our own. In addition, we examined the battles facing our family's eternal souls. Let's take a moment to examine how we can become better equipped within our own lives, and the lives of those we nurture as we face these daily battles.

- During a typical day, how often do I intentionally consider how good or evil is working in my life?

- What keeps me from intentionally contemplating God or the devil in my life's circumstances?

- What are some examples of today's cultural views on God and religion? How have I been influenced to follow prevailing cultural beliefs?

- Why would the devil want to condition me into not thinking intentionally about him?

- What consequences of this sinful mindset have I witnessed in my life and in my family's lives?

- What vision did I lock in of the three concentric circles?

- Which circle do I believe is the most important and why?

- When I consider the smart people I admire most in the world, what qualities of intellect and reasoning stand out? Are we guilty by association?

- When is fantasy healthy? When is it unhealthy?

- How can I know with confidence what is true and virtuous? How can I develop this wisdom within my family?

- How do I exercise my free will toward God, or against Him, in my life?

- How has generations of manipulation led to a culture that now chooses, sometimes aggressively, to remove God from society?

- Can I clearly see where I have allowed sin to enter my life, and consciously work toward sinning no more?

- Do I understand the worth of my eternal soul and the souls of the family I nurture?

- What steps can I take today to strengthen my willpower and that of my family? How does the virtue of humility play a role?

- Do I understand the difference between a sinful mindset and falling to sin, and repentance through contrition?

Can we become competent to the fact that the choices we make lead us to our challenges and strengths? If we choose God's will, He will provide us with the strength needed to bring us through life's challenges. This is not something from which we can gain instant gratification. It takes willpower and commitment from within us to share in God's grace. Intention, composure, and humility are needed in our daily life to help us work toward our personal relationship with God in our spiritual life.

Challenge yourself to think daily about these newfound competencies and the effect they can have on the family you are or will be nurturing. If you are reading this book and sharing this experience within a men's group, commit to challenging each other and holding each other accountable to stay true to the path. We need the strength of living in the Word, rather than submitting to living in and of this world and having likeminded people around us to help us grow and create a foundation of faith within our families.

Become a witness to your own spiritual growth as it matures and as you become more intentional in your daily life. You will find yourself crossing paths more frequently with faithful servants and find yourself wondering if these encounters could be by chance. I assure you, the encounters are intentional. I call these events "God incidences."

Notes:

_____

_____

_____

_____

_____

_____

_____

_____

_____

_____

_____

_____

_____

_____

_____

_____

_____

Chapter 3
The Wedges of This World

It is faith that leads to God's grace. When you are in God's grace, truth and acceptance come naturally...

Let's identify how living in and of this world drives wedges through what is true and real, and cascades into all other aspects of our lives.

By this point, you have read the expression, "living in and of this world" more than a few times. As men, and especially as fathers, we need to be aware of what this means. We live in and of this world when we allow the physical and ideological world around us to diminish and suppress our spirituality. As we grow in faith and truly begin to understand the power of our own free will, we need to become competent in applying this expression and consciously incorporate it into our thoughts as we go through life. The world is filled with wedges that are intentionally placed to chip away at man's faith and separate him from what is true and real. We need to become diligent in identifying these factors in our lives.

This task is almost impossible for someone who is not actively working on his own personal relationship with God. If we are not truly conscious of our faith, and the worth of our soul, and the souls of the family we nurture, then "living in and of this world" becomes the norm. Sinful mindsets of deceit and selfishness become our accepted norms. They become the only way of life vastly known throughout the new generations. Our music and entertainment encourage this mindset. It fills our nightly news, delivered to us with a slanted viewpoint in a matter of fact tone. We're left with a mindset that accepts and shares attacks on traditional religion as if it were an outdated fanatical concept. Encouragement in self-indulgent sexual behaviors has become the accepted lifestyle, of no ill consequence, while sharing in an accepted sinful and subjective mindset. This behavior has settled deeply into the will and hearts of many who have been misled to acceptance of living in and of this world and the sinful mindset it perpetuates.

If we look closer, we will find that most people engage in such behaviors to make themselves feel whole, to fill a void deep within themselves, even if it is for only a moment. This realization is not competent to them. They are not consciously aware of this fact in their lives. This void, or longing, further leads to the need for instant gratification. Instant gratification comes in many forms – all of which lead to the practice of vice, not virtue. It is the constant chasing of instant gratification that leads us to many of the wedges that separate us from what is true and real. Over time, they also separate us from our will to be faithful.

Our children will know no other behavior or sense of being. They will never know the value of their eternal souls, without intentional fathers in their lives. We must first accept these facts in our own hearts and will and see them for what they are. As we grow in faith and truly own our own hearts, the wedges of this sinful world will become apparent. They will no longer have power over us, or the family we nurture. In fact, by continually chipping away at the wedges, we will gain the willpower needed to rise above our sinful nature and see clearly what is true and real through God's grace. Now, the world around us and the family we nurture are seen very differently. Make no mistake, this realization presents our free will with a difficult task. Our first step is to consciously accept that we are human and have a sinful nature, and that it is easier for us to look around, then choose to look away, and submit to falling short within our own humanity.

As we grow in faith and understanding, we gain the strength needed to chip away at the sinful nature and mindset that has become the norm in our lives. It is especially important for fathers, as heads of households, to see this clearly. It is easy to become overwhelmed by the reality of it all. With a clear perspective and realistic expectation, we can slowly work toward chipping away and removing the wedges that we all personally face.

As we remove each wedge, we begin to cooperate with grace. Grace leads us to the truth that fully satisfies our heart and will. But if we reject grace, then we casually submit to the temptations of the world to fill voids and longings that can never be filled in and of this world. Without accepting God's grace, this truth cannot be understood. Through expression of our own free will in the search for what is good and true, we begin to share in an intentional faith that leads to God's grace at work in us.

If you are actively working toward growing in faith, this task will become easier with each good decision made. The consequences of being complacent and living in and of this world have a domino effect on every other aspect of our lives. Working toward growing in faith, which develops our character simultaneously, will become evident to all around us.

At first, this may present uncomfortable changes in some of your relationships. Be aware of this realization. Stay intentional in your efforts. See the wedges for what they are. Like-minded people will cross your paths as you become more intentional in owning your faith. That is no coincidence. Such encounters will happen. God gives us only what we can handle. I cannot stress enough the point of being intentional in our daily lives. Faith leads to God's grace.

When you are in God's grace, truth and acceptance come naturally. Share this clarity within the family you nurture. Nurture the free will needed to fight the good fight for your family's souls every day.

Chapter 3 Study Guide
The Wedges of this World

In this chapter, we considered how the wedges of the world separate us from our spiritual destiny. We also looked at how this effect cascades into other parts of our lives. Let's explore these concepts more deeply.

- What does it mean to "live in and of this world" and what are some examples from my own life?

- What does faith mean to me and why is it important?

- What is grace? Do I share in it and how does it work in my life?

- What is the most important thing I can do to help my family understand the value of their eternal souls and spiritual lives?

- How can I arrange the time and opportunity needed to discuss with my own family some of the wedges of the world that threaten them? What might be the biggest obstacle to having these candid conversations?

- How can I use the difficult people and circumstances of my life like sandpaper to smooth out the rough edges of my faith journey?

- Who are the like-minded people God has sent into my life to help me and my family on our journey? Do I choose to let them in?

- Can I easily spot what is truly good in the world? Why or why not?

- How can I develop a stronger prayer life to feel the peace of the Father's presence in my life and to learn more about His deepest desires for me and my family?

My screen saver on my phone helps me stay focused in my daily life. It is a portrait of Christ on the cross. My youngest son Frank gave it to me, so it has a special meaning. It serves as a constant reminder of my need to face the cross in my daily decisions and actions. If I fall short, I face the cross and challenge myself to do better.

God's grace is the only way to achieve what we are all truly searching for, peace of mind. Instant gratification leads to a loss of willpower and self-worth, which cascades into all aspects of our lives. Face the cross and fight the good fight! I was once told that the only time we are truly at peace in this world, is when we are in prayer. We can all start there.

Notes:

_____

_____

_____

_____

_____

_____

_____

_____

_____

_____

_____

_____

_____

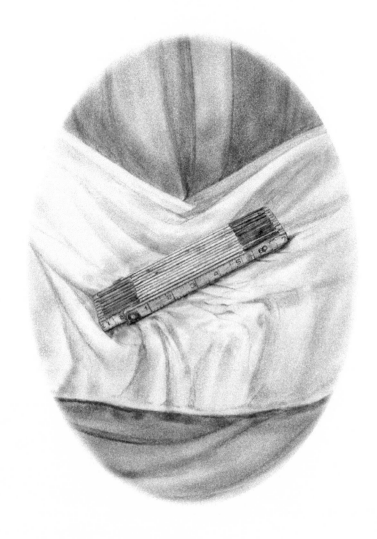

Chapter 4
Traditional Roles

Because the husband is the head of the wife, as Christ is the head of the church. He is the Savior of his body. Therefore, as the church is subject to Christ, so also let the wives be to their husbands in all things. Husbands, love your wives, as Christ also loved the church, and delivered Himself up for it.
~ Ephesians 5:21-25

In his letter to the Ephesians, St. Paul states that a man is to love his wife as Christ loves the Church. A woman is to be subject to her husband as to the Lord "because the husband is the head of the wife, as Christ is the head of the church" (Eph. 5:23).

What does this mean? Through the divine institution of marriage, man and woman become one. In fact, this union is so profound that it has been revealed to us through the Word of God to be a sacrament, a means by which God's grace is dispensed through the work of the Holy Spirit. As such, faith-filled husbands and wives submit their lives in a spirit of sacrificial love for the well-being of each other and for the procreation and upbringing of children – so that all may grow in faith and love to serve our Heavenly Father, as is intended for all God's children. In a similar way, St. Paul tells us that Christ is united to His Church for eternity. The Church draws its life from the Word and Body of Christ. Christ offers Himself entirely, to nurture His Church to grow in faith and love to serve our Heavenly Father.

When we consider marriage, in this way, we understand St. Paul's teaching that husbands imitate Christ when they offer themselves selflessly, humbly, and wholly to their wives in a spirit of unconditional love. When this happen, we see a love:

- that reflects compassion and an understanding of each other's faults

- that knows only of loving the other willingly through their faults

- so divine that it can only be shared in God's grace to be understood

- that is a true reflection of God's love and mercy for us all, worthy of the endless sacrifices needed

When we look around us do we see men worthy of this responsibility – men who truly know their place in the families they are supposed to nurture? Do we see men who know their place in their own lives?

Sadly, in today's world we see fewer and fewer men exhibit this kind of love. Rather, we see more examples of emasculated men whose self-indulgent, socially accepted behavior leads to careless relationships and unintentional fatherhood. The result has been an alarming increase in fatherless/husbandless homes, where men have forfeited their role as the spiritual head of their families. Some have abandoned their families altogether. Can you imagine what the Church would be like in the world without Christ to lead it and to serve it faithfully every day? There is a reason why God the Father sent His only begotten Son into the world; likewise, there is a reason why God established the role of husband/father within the family.

When husbands and fathers do not understand their God-given responsibilities within their families, women take on the role of head of the family. This often becomes a pattern that perpetuates to following generations. We see too many examples of single mothers struggling to make ends meet, while also trying to keep their children safe in a turbulent world. The world would have us believe that this non-traditional family is a perfectly acceptable social construct – and that many other non-traditional family structures are just as good, if not better than the natural construct of father, mother, and children. Society argues that we are wiser today than we were in St. Paul's time, and therefore we must view men and women as equal in every way. This argument is so pervasive that even the concept of *gender* becomes distorted and diminished in our modern culture.

Indeed, by God's design, men and women are equal in dignity and worth. But, the two genders are also, by nature, very different. These differences are good for the family. Because their bodies complement each other perfectly, men and women can bring new life into the world. Through the holy sacrament of marriage, husband and wife become one. Similarly, because God has bestowed men and women with unique spiritual gifts, husbands and wives can use these gifts in a complementary way to nurture their families and keep them grounded in God's grace. God made no mistake here. God gives men and women what they need to become truly one, in love and grace, to nurture faith-filled families that become forces for good in a chaotic world.

Over the decades, research has shown consistently that children raised within traditional households with both a father's and mother's influence are healthier and have fewer emotional and behavioral problems than children raised in other family structures.[4] This is not to say that exceptions do not exist; however, the essential truth is that children, raised within traditional family setting, are happier and better adjusted overall, and societies that support this basic principle are far better for it as a result.

Society, in general however, will deny the truth of the purpose for traditional families. Members of society attack the truth with malice and hate-filled accusations of male chauvinism. They disparage women who choose traditional roles as either weak or betraying the feminist cause. These people will label any argument in support of traditional families as intolerant. For those who live in and of this world, the truth is challenged with a sense of vengeance. The pursuit of the cause for tolerance consumes their lives, and ultimately separates them from God's grace. This poses torment in their search for their own personal relationship with God and has a cascading effect on their daily lives. Thus, God's Truth cannot settle into the will of the challenger.

So how can we objectively approach this subject with others when we bear the weight of such worldly labels as intolerance and hatefulness? To start, we can find truth through our own faith that leads to God's grace. When we see truth clearly for what it is – a sign of God's unconditional love for us – then we can live it courageously and act compassionately toward those who are struggling with the truth.

We do not want to mirror the malice that reflects from the dissident. We can try to offer suggestions that encourage him or her to seek the truth outside of the cause. This will indeed challenge the will and create a notion of uneasiness that often accompanies any consideration to change, which we all know is difficult. It is a natural human emotion to become offensive and reject change. We must know this going in and be mindful of the need for composure when confronting the dissident's reality. If the dissident is a loved one, then sharing the truth can take on a different meaning. Challenging loved ones with the truth can be painful and shake our own faith at times. But God is a loving Father who desires all His children to be saved. One can realize this truth only in the state of grace, where our hearts and minds are free of sin and in full communion with the loving God who made us. Faith leads to love.

Demonstrating the selflessness and humility needed to rightfully take on the traditional roles of husband and father (and wife and mother) is a tremendous responsibility – and requires great courage today. Staying in the Word, rather than living in and of the world, will help us become competent to the commitment needed. For the faithful, through God's grace, the family is seen clearly and is defined solely as a father, mother, and children. Any manipulation of this natural fact stands outside of God's will.

We must remain dedicated to staying true to our own faith. We must commit ourselves to helping our loved ones understand the value of their souls and the importance of living the faith that leads to God's grace. Through humility and composure, we must be able to respect different positions. Yet, we still must summon the willpower needed to share the truth in a selfless and loving way that shines a light on the value of every human soul. With the aid of God's grace and a compassionate heart, we can truly learn to love the sinner and hate the sin – and most of all, to know the difference.

Chapter 4 Study Guide
Traditional Roles

Within this chapter, we gained an understanding of God's view and the worldly view of traditional roles as they apply to our families. Let's explore these views as they relate to the families we nurture. Let's focus on becoming competent to the importance and impact of this reality on our journeys to be better husbands and fathers.

- Am I aware of God's place for me within my family? Why or why not?

- Who are the men in my life who helped me understand my role, as God intended, and who provided a clear example of how to fulfill this role within my family?

- Where in my life can I do a better job of becoming competent to the commitment required to be an intentional husband and father?

- How does St. Paul's comparison of Christ's love for the Church with a husband's love for his wife help me understand how I should relate to my wife within my family?

- What does my relationship with my wife teach my children about God's love for them?

- What are some examples of the chaos in the world resulting from the breakdown of traditional marriage and the family?

- How can we recognize, with crystal clarity, the perversions of traditional roles about men, women, and marriage in the world and the trumpeting of false causes that so many have accepted into their will?

- How can I show my family (and others) that God is not mistaken in His design of man, woman, and the institution of marriage?

- What is necessary to ensure that we do not mirror the malice reflected by those who accuse us of intolerance and hate?

As we reflect on these questions, the challenges they present to our lives and the lives of our loved ones may seem overwhelming. The most important point to keep in mind is to accept the lessons learned from our past and to move forward in a spirit of trust and reconciliation. Through our Father's merciful love for us, we are invited to enter a state of grace, where our hearts and minds are in full communion with the loving God who made us. Through humility and faith, we can chip away at the sinful nature that separates us from God's grace. Knowing and focusing on the worth of our soul, and the souls of our loved ones, can settle deeply into our will and provide the strength needed to fight the good fight in our daily lives.

Notes:

_____

_____

_____

_____

_____

_____

_____

_____

_____

_____

_____

_____

_____

_____

_____

_____

_____

_____

_____

Chapter 5
Owning Your Own Faith

Bitterness is the lingering taste left behind from life lessons not learned. A bitter person is one who never recognizes loss as an opportunity to grow. The greater the loss, the more opportunity we have to learn and to grow. Pride keeps us from learning our lessons in our youth. Humility is our professor throughout our lives. Wisdom is our course. It's easy to recognize the honor students among us. Some people, however, never even show up to class...

Those of us who were born into a Catholic family are known as "cradle Catholics," meaning we were immersed in the teachings of the faith from the time of our infancy. No one is born with a full knowledge of God, as our Father, and a clear understanding of our role as His beloved children. We must be given this information in doses appropriate to our level of understanding, little by little.

For many of us cradle Catholics, we learned our faith as children in Catholic schools, or via other religious instruction. At a young age, our faith formation often took on the same level of meaning as our math and science classes. But there was something greater at work in the depths of our subconscious at this time in our lives – when learning and discovery were the objects of the day. While discovering our faith, we experienced the graces of Baptism, Reconciliation, Eucharist, and Confirmation. Although we may not have fully understood God's saving grace at such a young age, we nonetheless received it. For it is through these sacraments that we receive God's saving grace through the work of the Holy Spirit. A foundation of faith was built through the sacraments that we received. The gathering of families participating in multiple, faith-filled sacramental celebrations added immeasurable value to our own foundation of faith. In fact, more than our faith was formed at this time of our lives. The development and nurturing of our moral compass and posture were in the hands of our parents at this crucial point in our development.

Without even recognizing it, our faith formation challenged us to think of such moral concepts as *accountability* and *choices*. These experiences contributed to molding virtue and moral posture into our will – all of which help promote a lifelong capacity for good decision making. This holds true for all who received their sacraments, regardless of the parenting received. Unintentional parents, who practice only a rote Catholicism, usually do not begin to make the conscious decision to intentionally nurture their own faith, until later in life after many hardships lead them back to the faith.

Many young adults today are choosing to step away from their Catholic faith. They truly do not understand the meaning of owning their own faith and the consequences their choices will have on their families. I believe many of these young adults were never challenged with the notion of owning their own faith as children. They just borrowed the rote faith of their unintentional parents. Now, as these young adults start families of their own, they see no value in the sacraments they once received, and they choose not to pass on the sacraments to their own children. For the children, the absence of the sacraments in their lives will pose challenges that they (and their unintentional parents) can hardly begin to comprehend.

The foundation of faith, received through preparing for and sharing in the sacraments, provides a subconscious moral compass that helps children navigate through life's lessons. The young parents who see no value in passing on the sacraments to their families unknowingly expose their families to great risk. By the time such parents encounter the difficult life lessons that lead them toward greater wisdom and faith, they discover it is too late in life to instill these lessons learned in their children. For these parents, a deep regret is inevitable as they watch their children grow weak in faith and make decisions that separate themselves from God's grace. Through their parents acceptance of, and the worldly reflection of significant others in their lives, and the external influence of the elite media and other social forces, these children choose to live in and of this world. Those weak in faith are more likely to submit to the worldly view and fall away from the truths of God's grace, without any recognition of what they have lost. They will unwittingly trade the "pearl of great price"

(Matt 13:46) for a piece of gravel and consider themselves wise and wealthy for it.

Unintentional cradle Catholics must become knowledgeable of the value of sharing in the sacraments. Such knowledge leads to a foundation of faith that enables one to share in God's grace. Unintentional cradle Catholics must learn how to own their own faith. For example, do you see the sacraments as merely symbolic, sentimental traditions? Or do you see them for what they truly are as spiritual rebirths? Through the sacraments, we come into the fold of a loving Father who fills us with His powerful, saving grace so that we can learn how to endure and face the challenges of this world while always being mindful of the world to come. How you answer this question is critical. There is a profound difference between experiencing our faith and owning it. It is only when we can answer this question with the latter thought in mind, that we truly come to own our faith.

For those who do not understand the difference, life's journey takes a more uncertain path. The longing for acceptance in this world leads many to focus on self-defined truths and just causes that cast doubt on Church teachings. Worldly dissidents are quick to perpetuate examples of the sinful nature of the Church's members and hierarchy to firmly place wedges between Catholics and their faith, or between Catholics and other Christians for that matter. The development of many Christian denominations, separated from the Catholic (Universal) Church, is another trumpet blast used by dissidents to confuse the weak of faith and to provoke doubt, which adds to the weakening of Christianity as a whole. The only element of truth that should be recognized in such shrill trumpeting is that we are all sinners. The Church is made up of sinful people who constantly need to be reminded who their Savior is, as well as the need for salvation. If we doubt this, all we need to do is consider the imperfections of the 12 apostles chosen by Jesus Himself.

Anyone who searches sincerely and humbly for the fullness of truth ultimately will be led by the Holy Spirit to the Catholic Church. The one, holy, catholic, and apostolic Church is not all these things because of the oppressive efforts of powerful men over generations of time. It is because of the sacrificial offering of Jesus Christ, who established the Universal Church to fulfill the will of His Heavenly Father, who desires all to be saved. The Church exists in the world like a rescue ship navigating the dark, stormy waters to save those lost at sea. The ship is kept on course by a series of captains (or popes), beginning with Saint Peter. With each successive pope, the mission of the Catholic Church continues. There is no denying the historical validity of this truth.

But this truth will only become evident to those who own their faith; that is, those who make the effort daily to live and understand their faith.

As we look around at the weak of faith and their families, it is easy to see their struggles. Fathers not understanding their rightful place add to and perpetuate the suffering of our worldly families. The "feminine-less" view of women's equality confuses our daughters and discourages them from exploring and finding their own will and worth. The worldly view now is that a princess is stronger without a prince. Is that truly a healthy thought for a developing little girl? Independence at all costs is the message that society is singing into her subconscious and into the minds of all our children. What is settling into the depths of their hearts and will as a result? It is surely not an appreciation for or an understanding of traditional families and values.

All who live in and of this world are choosing to separate themselves from God's grace and from their rightful place at His table. Do we not recognize the resulting sufferings from lost or fractured faith foundations within our own families and their cascading effects?

With intent, we can nurture our own personal relationship with God, which leads us to resting peacefully in grace and clarity of truth. Our daily pursuit of owning our own faith will be seen by God in all that we do. We will feel His reflection of love for our efforts in our hearts. This reality will strengthen our wills so that our efforts may be aligned to fight the good fight as we continue to rise above our sinful nature.

Chapter 5 Study Guide
Owning Your Own Faith

In chapter 5, we explored "owning our faith." For those of us born into the Catholic faith (cradle Catholics), we look at our Catholic upbringing and its worth as we developed from childhood through adolescence into adulthood. Let's explore how preparing for, and sharing in, the sacraments helps us build a foundation of faith that leads to virtuous decision making throughout all of life. We look at how living in and of this world leads many to fall away from their faith and to form self-defined truths that cast doubt on Church teachings. And we look at how all these facts combined cascade into the families we nurture.

- What contributes to making cradle Catholics "weak of faith"?

- What doubts do I carry about the sacraments and Church teachings? What efforts do I make to learn the truth behind these teachings? What sources of information do I turn to?

- When I go to Mass, do I see families who I perceive to be living the sacraments and owning their faith? What does this look like?

- How do the sacraments play a valuable role in developing the faith foundation of my family? As a husband/father, how can I improve the way I live and reflect on the sacraments within my own life and my family's?

- How does the loss of God's grace, dispensed primarily through the sacraments, lead to suffering in the world?

- What roles do fathers and mothers play within the family? What happens when these roles are confused or forfeited? What is the cascading effect upon the family from one generation to the next?

- Is the Catholic Church holy? Why? What makes it holy?

- Can we accept that we are all sinners, and the Church, while inherently holy, is made up of imperfect people? Can we see the truth in the Church's teachings? Why or why not?

- What makes something true? What happens when we lack clarity of truth?

- Do we fully understand the value of owning our own faith, and how this cascades into the lives of the families we nurture? From this point forward, how can I do a better job of owning my own faith?

Living in and of this world creates daily challenges that threaten our faith and weaken our will. Being able to recognize the challenges that form wedges between ourselves and our faith is our first line of defense toward owning our faith. Being intentional and focusing on the effects of the choices we make as they relate to our faith will become an automatic practice; an unconscious competence, after only a few weeks of conscious intent. Sharing in the reward of making good choices will make each decision easier, as we progress in our daily efforts to own our faith. God will see our intent toward composure. The strength to persevere will present itself, as the truth of God's grace, seen and reflected in our daily life. Choose to face the cross.

Notes:

_____

_____

_____

_____

_____

_____

_____

_____

_____

_____

_____

_____

_____

_____

_____

_____

_____

_____

_____

_____

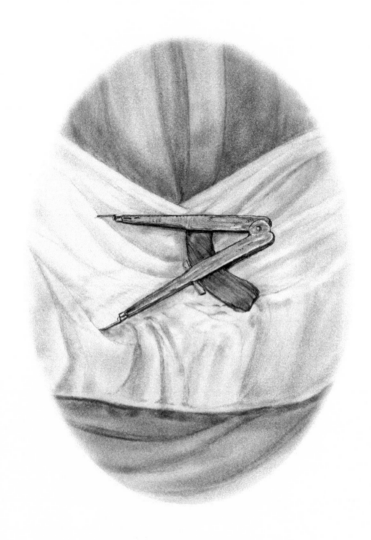

Chapter 6
The Arch of Life

If we are not working toward our spiritual journey, then we are
stepping away from it...

Anyone who takes a journey knows that its success depends upon many things, but most assuredly it depends upon a firm foundation. Without firm ground to tread upon, we risk losing our footing or sustaining an injury, which can slow our progress or end our journey prematurely. Our spiritual journey is no different.

Envision the spiritual journey in the framework of "the arch of life," an immense majestic steadfast arch, the span of which is reinforced and bound together on both ends by God's grace.

Let's consider that the spiritual journey has three stages, each of which has varying degrees of self-awareness about one's own faith – the first being *apprentice*, followed by *journeyman*, and, finally, *master carpenter*. This third stage calls to mind the trade that was handed down from St. Joseph to Jesus, just as our faith is handed down from our heavenly Father to us. Let's look at our spiritual journey as "the arch of life" and consider how it applies to the lives we lead.

Apprentice

Cradle Catholics, typically learn the faith in a classroom setting. We are apprentices of the faith; learning the beliefs and practices that make us part of the faith community. If our faith is not nurtured in a way that leads us closer to God's grace during this important period of spiritual growth, we will forever stay weak in faith in the apprentice stage of our spiritual journey. We will not experience the fullness of truth about our faith that only sharing in God's grace can make clear.

We have two ways to start our apprenticeship. The first is through a faith-filled family of intentional parents partaking in the sacraments. If we are fortunate enough to have intentional, faith-filled parents, those faith-filled gifts are handed on to us in a way that points us toward true north on our moral compass. This path builds a firm foundation of faith, from which springs a lifetime of conscious moral decision making. The second way to start our apprenticeship is later in life, when some event causes us to draw near to Our Lord. Weak in our faith, we come to realize that we have been misdirected on our journey by unwittingly following the many false causes of those living in and of this world.

Both paths require us to chip away at our sinful nature and fight the temptations that living in and of this world leads to, particularly for the weak of faith. Whether we begin the arch of life in our parents' care or as adults, we are in the apprentice state of the journey, easily formed by virtue or vice.

Journeyman

The transition from apprentice to journeyman begins with a disposition of humility and an awareness that God is the true moving force for good in the world. The eager-to-learn apprentice is tested through many trials that living in and of this world present. Apprentices who do not start their journey on firm footing can become blind to the truth by the many different apparently good causes that this world wedges between them and their faith. They are also blind to the fact that they separated themselves from God's grace and therefore are unable to clearly see the truth. The worldly cause becomes their focus and their concept of truth.

If we choose to face the reality that God is the true moving force for good in the world, and if we work past the daily wedges that present themselves, then we will find ourselves within the spiritual awakening period of our journey. Choosing to nurture our faith is the beginning of owning our own faith. The journeyman stage shares in God's grace. The sacrament of Reconciliation provides the strength needed to come into the full awareness of God's grace. Understanding the realization of this truth adds to the strength needed to be intentional while chipping away at the sin that presents itself in our daily lives along the journey.

There is no better realization than sharing in the truth seen clearly in God's grace. Does this change the way we view the people around us? Does our spiritual awakening change the way the people around us view us, as our faith presents itself in our lives? Living in God's grace inevitably leads to more challenges that living a faith-filled life presents. But being conscious and aware of God's grace challenges us to rise above our sinful nature and to stay in the truth. We expect that our spiritual journey will fill us with a loving desire to seek and to learn about our faith daily, just as we expect to grow daily in our personal relationships and work lives. Seeking the Word and pursuing the grace that leads to a varying awareness of faith in our daily lives are representative of the journeyman period of our spiritual journey.

Master Carpenter

As the years of our intentional spiritual journey bring us closer to the realization of God's grace and the truth it provides, we find ourselves in the master carpenter stage. It is in this period that we find ourselves resting naturally and competently in the truth that God's grace has shown to us during the arch of our spiritual journey. We now possess the tools to share with others as they journey through the apprentice and journeyman stages of faith. The choices we made along the way in our daily attempts to chip away at the sin within and around us led us to a truly faith-filled existence. We can now easily identify the wedges of sin as they present themselves in our daily lives

As a master carpenter, we see good and evil clearly, and no longer submit to living in and of this world. We understand that no worldly cause is worth giving up our soul or compromising our reception of God's grace. Our willpower and our intentional efforts strengthen us and the families that we nurture, so that we may live the faith to the best of our worldly ability. This stage provides us with the peace of mind to ready us as good and worthy servants for our day of judgment.

Accept, reconcile, and face your faithful journey daily so that you can rest in union with God's grace and truth. If we are not working toward our spiritual journey, then we are stepping away from it. Do not be misled. There is no middle ground. Every journey starts with one step. For most of us, our responsibility to others and their journeys relies on the reflection of faith seen through the lives we lead, as we live in the truth of God's grace. Accept and own the responsibility of handing on faith-filled gifts to the family you nurture so that you can lead your family sure-footedly through the arch of life.

A Prayer for the Journey

Our journey through the arch of life is often described as a battle, and the good and worthy servant who intentionally enters that battle (whether an apprentice, journeyman, or master carpenter) is a warrior of Christ. Chipping away at the wedges of vice and false virtue in the world is truly a daily battle. We must fight the good fight every day to remain firmly grounded in the truth of God's grace.

Here is a prayer that every Christian warrior should use to overcome the temptations of sin.

Prayer to Saint Michael the Archangel

Saint Michael the Archangel, defend us in battle. Be our protection against the wickedness and snares of the devil. May God rebuke him, we humbly pray; and do thou, O Prince of the heavenly host, by the power of God, cast into hell Satan and all the evil spirits who prowl about the world seeking the ruin of souls. Amen.

Take time to seek out the origins of this powerful prayer for valor. Anyone who recites this prayer daily, along with three Hail Mary's, in a spirit of humility and true contrition, will surely find the discernment needed to fight sin and to see the world around them clearly. Aside from the Blessed Trinity, I believe that our Blessed Mother, St. Joseph and Saint Michael are three of the most powerful forces in the Universal Church. Calling upon their intercession in all your spiritual battles is a great starting point to owning your own faith and advancing sure-footedly through the amazing journey of the arch of life.

Chapter 6 Study Guide
The Arch of Life

In chapter 6 we explore the concept of the "arch of life" and the foundation that supports it. By embracing the stages of the arch of life, we become aware of the:

1. Idea of looking at our faith journey in different stages and examining the benefits and struggles within them.

2. Daily struggle of sin.

3. Benefit that living an intentional faith-filled life leads to overcoming the challenge of sin and we rest peacefully in union with God's grace.

Let's now challenge ourselves on how these competencies affect our daily life and the lives of the families that we nurture.

- What are the different stages of faith in the arch of life and what are some examples of the daily spiritual struggles that we face within each stage?

- Why do many people remain in the apprentice stage?

- What will we fail to attain if we stay in this stage?

- How do parents influence the path by which their children enter and grow beyond the apprentice stage?

- What is good moral posture and how do intentional fathers reflect it? Why is this an important element of a child's faith foundation?

- What is truly missing from the lives of those who feel that they are missing something in life?

- What sacrament can serve as a powerful channel of God's grace in the journeyman stage? How have you experienced this?

- Describe a high point in your own personal faith journey where you clearly saw the truth of God's grace in your life.

- How would you describe the true value of your soul and the souls of the family you nurture? How do your daily efforts rise above your own sinful nature to reveal the truth of the soul's value?

- What is required to become a master carpenter? How does the master carpenter relate to God and to others?

- What day is the master carpenter ready for?

- If we are not working toward our personal relationship with God, what are we working toward?

- Why is it easier to be tempted by vice than virtue while living in and of this world? Whose intercession can assist us especially in the battle against sin?

- At what stage of the arch of life do you find yourself right now? Explain.

For me, the theory of "the arch of life" presents a clear perspective of how to build a solid foundation of faith within our own lives and the lives of the families we nurture. This theory also provides a clear perspective of the elder stage, the master carpenter, who is worthy of striving for that spiritual place deep within; where one rests peacefully in the truth of God's grace and is no longer challenged by the wedges that living in and of this world presents. By receiving God's grace and reflecting a good moral posture, gained through the many years of living an intentional, faith-filled life along the journey, we can now easily direct our free will to the best of our worldly ability to nurture and guide the families for whom we are responsible. The concept of the "arch of life" provides us with a competency for a life and reality worth fighting for!

Arch: a curved structure, especially one that supports a building or a bridge.[5]

For our purposes, an arch is a bridge supporting one's journey from this world to the next. Enjoy the journey of a lifetime... your journey!

Notes:

_____

_____

_____

_____

_____

_____

_____

_____

_____

_____

_____

_____

_____

_____

Chapter 7
Perception is Reality

For those of you who give spiritual scandal, it is better to tie a
millstone around your neck and throw yourself in the ocean.
For those of you who receive and accept religious scandal, it is
surely spiritual suicide.

~ Matthew 18:6-7

The process of perception becoming reality takes little time to settle into our will. Often, we require little intellectual effort to move from a first impression to a deeply held truth, or a situational truth. Look around at what society now accepts as our new norm. Many of today's currently perceived "truths" were viewed as outright falsehoods 50 years ago, 10 years ago, even four years ago. Somewhere along the spectrum of time the standard for critical thinking changed, and the situation now drives our moral decision-making, rather than objective truth. Today, society encourages us to define reality, or truth, based on our perception of what feels right in a given situation through the lens of what society accepts.

Can truth really change because one's perceptions or feelings change? Can 2+2 equal 5 simply because one's perception of the value of numbers suddenly changes? If everyone's perception is an acceptable reality, based on the way society perceives a situation, then what value or role does truth play in our world?

Today's culture is on a dangerous path. When an apparent truth dramatically changes, only one of two things is logically valid. Either the reality of truth was originally misinterpreted, or the changed perception is and always will be false. How do we determine which is which? How hard are we willing to work to engage the intellectual rigor required to find absolute truth? For cradle Catholics, a great place to start is to examine how the world perceives the Church and the Mass today.

Those living in and of this world tell us repeatedly that the Catholic Church is intolerant and outdated; its authority is unjust; its sacraments are dead traditions; its form of worship, the Mass, is dull and meaningless. Yet, this is the same Catholic Church that Jesus Christ handed down through the generations as a precious gift. How could Jesus Christ, the Eternal Living Word, leave us with a finite, dead relic? What logical sense does that make? Yet, for many who live in and of this world, it is an easy perception to accept, when they perceive the Catholic Church as separate from Jesus Christ. Those living in and of this world find a sense of personal satisfaction through instant gratifications. It is easy to conform to the whims of the world, which change like the wind. However, living a solid life of faith, in conformity with God's will, takes effort. The promises of the world satisfy for a moment, triggering a ravenous hunger that always leaves us looking for more.

In today's culture, how can the Mass compete with the charismatic preacher who grabs hold of the heartstrings of cradle Catholics, still living in the adolescent stage of their faith journey? With a backdrop of light shows and music, our brother in Christ preaches feel-good messages that are all about the congregation and their daily struggles. Life is difficult (we can all agree on that), The preacher shows compassion, offers helpful suggestions, and reassures our brothers and sisters in Christ, that the only effort they need to make "to be saved" is to accept Jesus Christ into their lives as their personal Lord and Savior. For our Protestant brethren, faith alone is all that is required! This perception of salvation becomes a welcome and easy reality for some cradle Catholics who experienced a different reality; a reality that involved lifelong traditions built from living a sacramental life, which they never grew to fully understand.

But is the perception of justification by *faith alone* a theological reality? Is that what is taught in Romans 3:28, which is the Protestant proof text for this perception of salvation, along with Ephesians 2:8-9, which states that salvation is through the grace of God and not because of works? Our Protestant brothers and sisters view these biblical passages as the primary basis for their arguments against the Catholic Church as a "flawed" religion. In truth, however, these passages begin to reveal the truths of the Catholic Church and its teachings for us all.

If we consider the totality of the Bible, we find that justification by faith alone is not stated anywhere in Scripture. Romans 3:28 does not contain the word, alone, in any Bible prior to the Reformation. Justification from the time of Abraham, onward, was never meant to be a one-time event (cf. James 2:14-26). Justification in the New Covenant begins at Baptism (cf. John 3:5) and is lived throughout one's entire sacramental life. Jesus instituted the sacraments of Baptism (cf. Matthew 3:13-15, 28:18-20), Reconciliation (cf. John 20:21-23), Confirmation (cf. Acts 2:1-4, 8:14-24), Holy Eucharist (cf. Matthew 26:26-29, 1 Corinthians 11:23-32), Holy Matrimony (cf. Matt 19:6), Holy Orders (cf. Matt 16:18, 1 Peter 5:1-4), and Anointing of the Sick (cf. James 5:14-15). Little effort would provide many more Bible references on the sacraments. A faith-filled life, lived through a healthy understanding of the New Covenant and the sacraments, helps us respond to God's call to take our rightful places at His heavenly table. This sanctifying grace that I speak of is a free and undeserving gift from God the Father. Specifically, the sacrament of the Eucharist, provides us with the spiritual food and stamina we need to persevere in the world and to reach our eternal salvation. In the Eucharist, Jesus fulfills His promise to be with us always and to keep us safely in communion with Him as we work out our salvation (cf. 2 Peter 1:3-11).

Consider also, our Protestant brothers' second proof text, used to find fault in the Catholic Church: Ephesians 2:8-9 states that it is by grace we are saved, through faith, and not by any works on our part. However, if you read the next verse, you find that St. Paul tells us that we are God's great work of art, created by Jesus Christ for good works. St. James also tells us faith without works is dead, and it is by works of love, and not faith alone, that we are justified (James 2:24-26). Jesus Christ warns us that not everyone who speaks the name of the Lord and believes in Him will be saved (cf. Matthew 25:31-46).

If we follow the premise that we are justified by faith alone, then we cut ourselves off from the immense and powerful gifts of the sacraments that Jesus Christ gave us to lead us to grace and eternal salvation. If we drift away from the Mass and follow the easy allure of a path to salvation paved with flashy light shows, uplifting music, and dramatic preaching, then we will gratify our senses, momentarily, but risk losing a lifetime of full communion with Christ. Over time, we unwittingly find ourselves committed to culture and not to Christ.

Intentional Catholic parents need self-composure, compassion and humility to honor God in the sacrifice of the Mass, nurture the faith foundation of the family, and allow the family to receive the Mass' spiritual gifts. We rarely see such moral posture reflected in the world today. Society fights hard to intentionally perpetuate the false perception that the Mass is a dead tradition; boring and detached from reality. But here is the key to understanding the true value of the Mass. The celebration of the Mass is not meant to be about us! How many cradle Catholics, living in the adolescent state of faith, recognize the fact that the Mass has been built and assembled around the Eucharist over the last 2000+ years? The Mass was built as the means for gathering to commemorate Jesus' perfect sacrifice, the ultimate sacrifice, by which no further blood sacrifices are necessary in the New Covenant

The re-presentation of Jesus' perfect and ultimate sacrifice is the main event and main objective of the Mass' gathering. The Mass culminates when the ordained priest offers up the sacramental sacrifice of bread and wine. The Holy Spirit then turns the bread and wine into the true Body and Blood of Christ, the Eucharist, through the miracle of transubstantiation. The word *Eucharist* means a gift of thanksgiving! This sacrificial offering is our free response to Jesus' command to "do this in remembrance of me" (Luke 22:19). The nourishment and fulfillment we receive in the Eucharist is for all of God's children to share in weekly, if not daily. This spiritual food enables His children to stay "in union" (i.e., communion) with Him, their loving Father.

For those who do not take the time to understand the parts and meaning of the Mass, the routine and repetitive nature of it may leave them wanting for more. What could be better than receiving the Body, Blood, and Divinity of Christ and then taking that amazing grace out into the world? Yet, incredibly, if we do not put forth the effort to grow into owning the faith handed down to us through the Church by apostolic succession, then we will sadly submit to societal norms and choose trend over Sacred Tradition. We will trade a sacramental life that leads to God's favor, for worldly causes.

As parents, we naturally want to see our children happy. We want to embrace those experiences that generate the greatest levels of comfort and satisfaction. When one begins the process of stepping away from the Catholic Church and the sacraments, in pursuit of instant gratifications, one will not see right away the tragic loss of the foundation of faith within their families. The loss of the foundation of faith presents itself in future generations. Parents who shared in this foundation but practiced only a rote Catholic faith, recognize that their children's and grandchildren's struggles are the result of a fractured faith foundation. Fathers, become aware of this fact. Recognize the wedges, placed firmly within this world to separate us and our families from God's favor, from what is true and real, and from the sacramental life handed down to us by Jesus Christ. Anything worthwhile comes from effort. Our families are worth the effort.

The foundation of faith and morality that settles into the heart and will of the child of intentional parents can only be seen through sharing in God's grace. This foundation cannot be built from the instant gratification of today's trends. These trends support many false causes through misleading statements, such as "We want to be known for what we are for, and not for what we are against...." Such distorted statements lead the misguided further away from objective truth by appealing to their sense of compassion.

The only way that we can see objective truth is through God's grace. This objective truth helps us to know the difference between apparent truth and truth itself.

As human beings, when we are too close to something, then it becomes hard to see the truth. Often a lifetime of poor choices will inhibit the possibility of seeing the truth. Over time, we will come to see the truth in our past choices, for better or worse. We will see the futility of living in and of this world and realize the true beauty of God's promises. But, if we reject God's gift of salvation, then we and the generations that follow will lose much. Consider what the culture has already lost in just the last 10 years in terms of morality and family values. The choices that we make now will affect the lives of our loved ones for generations to come. If we, as fathers, do not choose to diligently fight the good fight, what will the next generation's perception of truth/reality look like?

It is never too late to begin again, to strengthen the will, and to chip away, intentionally and continuously, at making the choices that challenge us to see things for what they truly are. If we are willing to challenge ourselves to think differently than the societal norm, then the growth we gain from truth will help us make good choices as we move forward. Through reflection and composure, we can examine the choices we made that caused us to fall short and unwittingly trade Sacred Tradition for a worldly trend.

If we turn to God to help us at understanding and accepting our sinful nature and to guide us in our efforts to rise above sin in our daily lives, then the truth will present itself clearly. We can separate ourselves from sin, just not from our sinful nature. Acceptance of this fact will lend itself as a tool that we will reach for and use daily. This tool will help us see our true self-worth as beloved sons and daughters of the Father.

When we reside in a state of grace, we see clearly the difference between truth and the false perceptions that have become the reality of truth, or situational truths, for many of those living in and of this world. Our first breath in the state of grace reveals our true worth in God's eyes and our rightful place at His table where we receive the sacrament of the Eucharist, shared within the celebration of the Mass. We see clearly that true compassion is the unconditional love expressed when we offer up prayers for those living in and of this world. We pray for those compelled by a false sense of need to take part in the many so-called worthy causes that separate them from the grace that makes truth clear. A confused state of reality awaits those who live outside of God's grace. Be diligent in recognizing the wedges that pull the misguided further away from God. Above all, recognize that clarity of truth leads to compassion for all of God's children. Love the sinner, but clearly see the sin.

So how should we approach those who made the choice to trade Sacred Tradition for trend, whether wittingly or unwittingly? Condemning and judging others in their faith journey and relationship with God is not the answer. The best response is to reflect love and compassion toward our brothers and sisters. Pray for clarity of understanding regarding the gifts revealed to us in the New Covenant and the sacraments. Choose to do good for them in a way that shares with them the path of God's love and mercy. Hopefully, that will bring them back to the bread of life shared in the sacrifice of the Mass. The Eucharist reflects as a true testament of our own faith. This, however, may be perceived as condescending to those good souls who traded tradition for trend, or for those among us who now find their truth through living for the cause.

This reaction is another wedge placed firmly to separate us from the revelation of truth. Remember, a false sense of compassion, pulling at our heart strings, is the wedge most used to separate us. Share this fact with others. I once listened to a homily where the priest turned to the altar boy and asked him his name, where he lived, where he went to school, and his parents' names. The priest then turned to the parishioners and changed all the facts that the boy just shared. He went on to tell the congregation that this is what we do in our own faith. We alter our perception of truth to a more palatable situational truth about our faith. These unconscious choices that the priest's illustration brought to light posed a challenge to the parishioners in attendance. Do we seek to live a faithful life that has the realization of God's will and grace? Or, do we choose to alter our faith to our own will and live for the moment or for the cause?

Yes, God is merciful and compassionate to those who choose to seek out truth and live in His grace. However, without a humble search for the truth, and remaining in God's grace, we cannot realize clarity of truth. There is nothing sadder to me than a good and worthy servant of God who attempts to depict God in his or her own image. With humble acceptance of God's truth, we can become competent in our own will to amend our own sinful ways. For some this might pose a torment greater than their will can withstand. Instead of surrendering joyfully to God's will and truth, they become opposed to the Church and trumpet false claims for the misguided to perpetuate. This adversarial perspective becomes part of their will.

Constant doubt supports a false sense of truth. This firmly places wedges between ourselves and reality. Elitist controlled social media and nightly news add to the perceived weakening of the Church, by perpetuating conflict through blasphemy. Here is where the family has an opportunity to do the work of God. The intentional father and mother take the time to explain the strongholds of elitism and impart truth to their children. In the state of God's grace, we realize the truth of God's Word and hand on with love and compassion, faith in God, not in man.

As fathers, we cannot sway from the daily commitment needed to intentionally nurture a faith-filled family in this world. We need to gain awareness that perception presents itself as reality to our children. They can easily be manipulated if we fail to intentionally nurture the foundation of faith within their hearts and wills. Where traditional authority is challenged and questioned, how can God's spiritual authority settle into the soul of a child? Especially when the child perceives that the father accepts the false perceptions and realities that govern the majority of those living in and of this world? Our obligation to our families is real, and our role as intentional fathers is critical. We need to take our rightful place within our family, so that our family can take its rightful place at the Eucharistic table of the Lord.

Let's try to imagine a world where the Church was never fractured; where:

- The Jews and Gentiles of Jesus' day followed His teachings as intended for us all.

- Humility would triumph over pride in society through virtuous free will.

- The Faith handed down to us was of the universal church that we all shared in.

- All of God's children live out the New Covenant and the sacraments.

If all the numerous, different denominations of Christianity are correct in all their teachings, then they are equally incorrect and cancel each other out. Truth is bright and visible; it is not corrupted by darkness.

It does not exist in many shades of gray. Can we see clearly the confusion that more than one perception of truth lends to the importance of them all? There is only one, holy, catholic, and apostolic Church that can be traced back in apostolic succession to Jesus' very hands. Truth is what sets us free. Don't take my word for it. Seek it out for yourself.

Here is a prayer, I penned, for unity within the Universal Church (meaning the Body of Christ both in heaven, purgatory and here on earth) that can be used as a petition for unity.

Prayer for Unity and Understanding for
All the Contrite Souls in Our Eternal Universal Church

Heavenly Father, through the power of prayers beseeched thee of the faith-filled families who have accepted Your Son, Jesus Christ, into their hearts and souls, and through the intercession of the communion of Saints above, unite and strengthen the will of all the contrite souls in the knowledge of, and acceptance of, your everlasting gift to us all, your eternal and all enduring Universal Church. We ask this, as we do all things, through Jesus Christ, our Lord. Amen.

For a good and worthy servant, this should be the perception of reality worth fighting for: Unity among all of God's children both in heaven and on earth, the Universal Church! We are all in this together. We all are meant to share in the same grace of undeserving favor of our loving Father. Lean into the Gospel.

Jesus said to them, "Amen, amen, I say to you, unless you eat the flesh of the Son of Man and drink His blood, you do not have life within you. Whoever eats My flesh and drinks My blood has eternal life, and I will raise him on the last day."
~ John 6:53-54

Chapter 7 Study Guide
Perception is Reality

In chapter 7, we explored how perception forms our sense of reality. We looked at how false perceptions form for those living in and of this world. We saw how these false realities firmly place wedges between the Universal Church and its members. We saw how the desire for instant gratification, aroused by cultural trends, leads many worthy souls away from their foundation of faith and from the fullness of truth that is seen clearly only through God's grace.

Fathers must become aware that false perceptions of truth will have negative consequences for future generations. This will impact those who do not share in the foundation of faith nurtured into the will of the family through the sacraments and the holy sacrifice of the Mass, the Eucharist. Let's focus on the competencies and intent needed to positively nurture our families on these facts.

- What is the cascading effect of spiritual scandal on the Church? Why does Scripture warn us against this sin?

- What effects of spiritual scandal have I observed in the world?

- What wedges do I form between myself and my foundation of faith when I take part in or help perpetuate religious scandal?

- How can I become competent to the importance of intentionally sharing and explaining God's truth to the family I nurture when spiritual scandal is identified?

- Where have I observed or experienced the worldly view that the Catholic Church is intolerant and outdated? Do I stand silent, or do I choose to challenge the claims?

- Am I aware that Jesus Christ gave the Catholic Church to the world as a gift? Do I understand what apostolic succession means? What sources do I rely on to form my (and my family's) understanding of this reality?

- Do I experience the celebration of the Mass as a sacrifice humbly offered up to God Himself? What cultural wedges try to diminish my understanding of this truth?

- How have I (or my family and friends) fallen prey to the appeals of trend over Sacred Tradition in a desire for instant gratification? How have I followed cultural trends to satisfy the will of my children? Why are children especially vulnerable to being swayed by false trends?

- How do the false compassionate cultural trends perceived as so-called truths create a false sense of family in the world? Why do such trends especially take aim at the traditional family construct that God designed for us all?

- What moral posture do I need to take to nurture a faith-filled foundation that is shared through the celebration of the sacraments, especially the Eucharist?

- How do the "feel-good" messages of some cultural trends create a false sense of compassion that leads us to fight for causes that ultimately separate us from God's grace? Why is it hard to recognize that we are stepping away from our faith when we align ourselves with such causes?

- How does praying for those who are separated from the faith inspire a true sense of compassion that reflects God's love and mercy? Why is prayer a more powerful force than judgment or condemnation?

- When have I practiced the call of all God's children to "love the sinner, but hate the sin"? How do I respond to that call continuously within the family I am responsible for nurturing?

- How can truth be situational? How has society imposed situational truths as absolute truth in our lives? How can we do a better job of identifying situational truths?

- As we move forward in our faith journey, can we understand how to separate ourselves from sin, while acknowledging our sinful nature? How do I struggle with this reality?

In our immoral world, some question and challenge the viewpoint of traditional values (and especially traditional roles within the family) as coming from small-minded, intolerant people. This perception lends a false reality to the many cultural trends. It causes many, who live in and of this world, to accept false realities as truth in their hearts and will. The family, and the traditional roles within it, holds a significant, rightful place in society and needs to be seen for the truth it represents. The faith-filled family rests peacefully in God's grace and enjoys a clarity of truth that reflects the love and mercy of God. The worldly point of view, on the other hand, which portrays the faithful as weak and intolerant, attempts to blind God's children to the truth and stir them to take up causes that separate them from God's grace. We need to embrace God's truth that leads to a true sense of compassion for all of God's children. We are called to love the sinner, see clearly the sin, and offer up prayers for clarity in the lives of those who have separated themselves from the faith.

We are all God's children, living in the arch of life at different places in our own personal journeys. The truest form of compassion we can offer this immoral world is to reflect God's love without judgment. It is up to the person with whom we speak to accept what we share with love. We are all accountable for our own actions. We are all responsible for owning our own faith. Pray for the clarity that leads to God's grace within the lives of the faithful living in and of this world who are now fighting for the false causes that have been presented to them as worthy. Be hopeful and rest easy in God's love for all His children.

Notes:

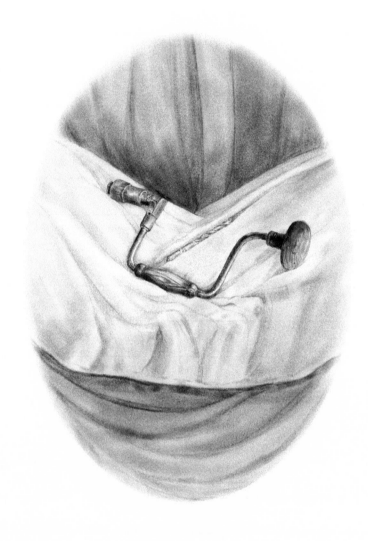

Chapter 8
Borrowing a Rote Faith

Rote: A memorizing process using routine or repetition, often without full attention or comprehension; mechanical or unthinking routine or repetition; a joyless sense of order.

~ Merriam-Webster[6]

In chapter 5, we discussed how many cradle Catholics have borrowed a rote faith from their parents, who have also borrowed a rote faith from their parents, and so on. This behavior has become prevalent within the Catholic Church. This is partly due to the way Catholics learn the faith, primarily through faith formation classes. As Catholics, we learn our faith methodically, as we would math or science, and it takes on the same importance within our adolescent minds.

For the child who learned their faith in a rote fashion, history repeats itself. Through the cradle Catholic's introduction to the sacraments, the foundation of faith is built but in need of nourishment. For many, the sacraments are merely requirements that must be completed. As children go through the process of completing these requirements, they may begin to observe and share in a heightened feeling of faith. Especially on those special days when they receive the sacraments for the first time. This heightened feeling may also come through words and actions of parents, clergy, or faithful parishioners, who intentionally take the time to spiritually nourish the children receiving the sacraments. The children may also experience this heightened sense of faith when they share in the sacramental celebrations of other family members or close friends. Throughout their adolescent years, children may see many faith-filled examples around them. However, these experiences will not deeply impress them. Nor will they internalize the spiritual importance of these examples, unless they share and grow in faith daily beyond these special occasions, at the hands of intentional parents.

Let's consider, for example, the celebration of the Mass. The way the Mass is celebrated within the Church's calendar year is methodical and repetitive. This is by design. The Mass is an intentional offering of a most holy sacrifice – the Body and Blood of Jesus Christ – which is a liturgical practice that Jesus Himself created at the Last Supper and asked us to do in remembrance of Him. God understands that we need the weekly, if not daily, practice of the Mass to fortify us and keep us firmly and sure-footedly on the path that leads to eternal life. For the adult Catholic who does not own their own faith, and lacks understanding, the repetitive practice of the Mass seems boring rather than holy, empty rather than spiritually fortifying. Like the reception of the sacraments, the Mass becomes nothing more than a requirement or a rote practice.

One way to determine if you are practicing a rote faith is to examine how you feel when you say the words, "Thanks be to God" after the priest says, "Our Mass has ended; go in peace." Do you barely remember saying the words? Do you feel joyless? Are you glad Mass is over? If you answer yes to any of these questions, then why do you attend Mass at all? Are you living a habit without any depth of feeling behind it? How is this habit strengthening the hearts and souls of the families you nurture?

If this is our reality as cradle Catholics, then we need to examine how we got to this place. What are the worldly wedges that misdirect cradle Catholics from owning our own faith? Yes, the foundation of faith (via the introduction of the sacraments within the faith community) has been built within the will of young Catholics. But if we do not continuously nurture this foundation and reinforce it within family life, we will find no comfort in the rite of the Mass, or the repetitive cycle of the liturgical year. We will experience no joy as we enter or leave Mass, because our faith is not owned, but merely borrowed from unintentional parents.

It is not long before the wedges of this world assemble in full force around the weak of faith, trumpeting out false claims and casting doubt upon Church teachings. Now worldly causes present themselves as good within the lives of the young. They hear enticing false messages perpetuated as truths by those living in and of this world. They hear that the Church is filled with old, dead traditions of intolerant, small-minded people. The weak of faith are lured toward more modern, enlightened ways that promise greater physical, emotional, intellectual, and spiritual fulfillment.

Without regularly sharing in the sacraments and the Mass, the weak of faith stand separated from God's grace and the light of truth. They enter slowly and surely not into a state of enlightenment, but rather into an endarkenment that can eventually envelop them. The intentional faith-filled Catholic must become aware of the dangerous concept of borrowing a rote faith.

As children of our loving God, we are not forsaken. By God's merciful love and the prayers of the faithful, the weak of faith may one day realize their missteps and find their way back to God's grace and truth. Much will need to be restored within them as they find their way safely back to the truth shared within the one, holy, Catholic, and apostolic Church. Let us remember, we are all children of a loving Father. Doubt does not have to lead to despair. The way back is a clear path for those who recognize the truth and choose to pursue it. The way back starts with true contrition through the sacrament of Reconciliation. This is the great hope of faith. Therefore, we have joy.

Understanding these facts will make us more competent at handing on our faith-filled gifts within our families. Sharing this competency with the families we nurture will strengthen their faith foundation and their faith-filled growth. The loss of the sacraments by future generations of our families will lead to the loss of a true moral compass to discern good and evil. What is true and real can only be seen through an intentional faith nourished by God's grace.

Chapter 8 Study Guide
Borrowing a Rote Faith

In chapter 8, we explored the concept of borrowing a rote faith as it relates to the sacraments and celebration of the Mass. We read that many cradle Catholics have lost sight of the importance of the sacraments, the Mass, and the Church's calendar year because of the repetitive nature of these liturgical practices. Without taking the time and effort necessary to develop a true understanding of these sacred events, many Catholics step away from the faith in search of something more exciting or gratifying. Let's consider the implications of practicing a rote faith within the families we nurture.

- Do we fully understand the meaning of rote, and how it applies to our Catholic faith?

- Have we borrowed a rote faith from our parents? How do we know?

- How will our understanding of this competency strengthen our family's spiritual growth?

- Do we know Catholics who left the Church for other Christian denominations to feel "whole" or "fed"? What are they really searching for?

- Have we ever challenged our family members to "own their own faith?" What wedges of the world keep us from challenging our families in this way? What awaits future generations who walk away from their faith?

- How does God love those who seek Him, even if their journey is different from ours?

- What parts of the Mass touch our hearts, minds, and souls? Why?

- During what parts of the Mass do we tend to drift off and lose focus? Why is that the case, and how can we change our response?

- Do we know why the Church's liturgical calendar is organized the way it is? How does our understanding of the Church calendar year deepen our faith and our understanding of God's love for us?

- How can we help our families make their participation in the Mass and their living out of the sacraments within the Church's calendar year more meaningful?

When we borrow something, it is never ours to own, especially within the context of faith. Therefore, understanding the circumstances surrounding how many cradle Catholics can become rote in their faith is a powerful competency for an intentional father, when nurturing his family's faith foundation. Addressing the need for a deep-rooted faith will lead to a clear understanding of the Church's teachings on the New Covenant, the sacraments, and how to intentionally live a sacramental life.

One way an intentional father can strengthen a child's faith and moral compass is by sharing an understanding of the fullness of joy that should be felt when we respond with the words, "Thanks be to God," after the priest says the Mass has ended. To be able to say these words with authentic joy, one must truly understand and experience the love God has for us, as reflected through the Mass.

Being loved, or sharing in love, is the only way we can experience true joy in our lives. God loved us so much that he gave His only son, Jesus Christ, who offered the ultimate sacrifice of suffering and dying on the cross to forgive our sins to save our souls. Sharing this awareness of God's love and mercy will strengthen the family's foundation of faith and prevent the borrowing or practice of a rote faith. Fathers, intentionally share these facts with the family you nurture.

Notes:

_____

_____

_____

_____

_____

_____

_____

_____

_____

_____

_____

_____

_____

_____

_____

_____

Notes:

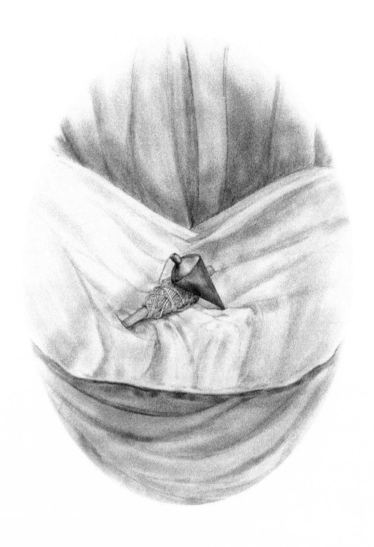

Chapter 9
Handing on Our Faith-Filled Gifts

If intentional parents consciously instill an understanding of the value of the sacraments within the families they nurture, then their children will unconsciously reflect a sound moral posture as they grow - even during the teenage years when the inclination to rebel and push away kicks in. Their children's moral compass will guide them and keep them on the right path...

For me, the thought of handing on our faith-filled gifts starts with the definition of the foundation of faith. My definition for the foundation of faith is very simple and can be summed up in two words: the sacraments.

I came to this realization – gradually – through my experience of living in a loving, faith-filled family who shared in the sacraments, and through my being a witness to my parents' steady moral posture throughout my childhood. Now, as I look back on my life and as I nurture my own family, I understand the powerful influence the sacraments impart on my faith journey.

While I always felt God's hand in my life, I see now that I was not always intentional in owning my own faith or handing it on to my family. I did not understand all the competencies associated with living the faith. I do believe that my experiences led me to this moment, where I can see clearly through God's grace and share these competencies, or tools, with you. What is now so clear is that children who partook of the sacraments live a life of moral principles and convictions that strengthen every aspect of their lives. Many cradle Catholics may unconsciously experience this truth, but it cannot be denied. I am proof of this fact.

If your child's physician tells you that your child is deficient in some essential vitamin, you will go to the drugstore to purchase that vitamin and ensure that your child takes it as prescribed. You do this because you trust the doctor and understand that without this vitamin, your child's physical health may deteriorate. As a result, your child might become exposed to greater health hazards down the road. We should view the sacraments in the same way.

The sacraments infuse our children with God's living grace, forming their moral conscience and safeguarding them from the dangerous trends and cultural hazards of living in and of this world. The sacraments enable them to thrive as God's beloved sons and daughters. Without the sacraments, they will surely experience a spiritual deficiency that will compromise their faith journey. If you are a father who received the sacraments, and you find no value in handing on these faith-filled gifts to the young family God has charged you with nurturing, what do you imagine will become of them? What happens to the child who enters adulthood without a strong faith foundation and without the moral compass that leads to good decision-making about important life choices? A word to the wise, it may be too late to protect your children from the consequences of living in and of this world without sharing in the sacraments, when you come to realize the value of the faith foundation that laid dormant within you throughout their adolescent years.

I came to this realization through my personal experience of observing the lives of families who either did not or do not currently share in the foundation of faith gained through the sacraments. I saw much pain and confusion in the lives of many good people (including cradle Catholics) who raise families outside of the Catholic faith. They do not possess the competencies necessary to understand how essential the foundation of faith is to weave a strong moral fiber throughout their children's lives, particularly in the adolescent years.

It is a father's responsibility to protect and safeguard his family. Accordingly, it is a father's responsibility to hand on the faith-filled gifts of the sacraments. The celebration of a sacrament shared strengthens the moral fiber, and the willpower of all family members in attendance. Why? Because the family is not just partaking of a sentimental faith tradition. It is truly experiencing, sharing, and receiving God's grace through the gifts of the Holy Spirit.

Understanding the value of the sacraments will make easier work for intentional parents who watch their children develop the moral posture so essential for making good life choices. For such parents, even when their children enter the teenage years, when the human emotion to rebel and push away is so strong, their children's moral compass will keep them on the right path. For loving Catholic parents, living a faith-filled life, always open to God's grace, deeply affects the way the family approaches life's challenges. The family with a strong foundation of faith can regard their struggles and the ways to solve them with greater clarity. They understand that God's grace is the only sure path to healing and restoration.

A firm foundation of faith will instill good intent in our children, and a healthy respect for others that will aid them as they find their way in the world. The idea that we are not the center of the universe is a liberating truth for children and adults alike. We are not islands unto ourselves. Rather, we are beloved members of the Body of Christ. Resting in God's love for us gives us peace of mind, as we raise our families and struggle through our physical lives.

I cannot stress enough the value of the sacraments in your own life and in the lives of the families you lead. As fathers, our daily pursuit of owning our own faith and handing it on to our families will be seen by God in all we do. His reflection of love for our efforts will be seen and felt through the moments of grace shared within our families. This will sustain us in our daily efforts to fight the good fight, as we continually rise above our sinful nature and selflessly hand on our faith-filled gifts.

The gifts of the sacraments form within us a powerful, life affirming force that keeps us joyfully on the path to eternal life. Let's review and reflect upon these awesome gifts that Jesus asks us to receive and to live, due to His great love for us and His longing to be with us forever.

The Seven Sacraments of the Catholic Faith

BAPTISM is necessary for salvation, cleansing us from Original Sin. With Baptism, we receive an indelible mark on our souls, marking us as belonging to God. We become adopted sons and daughters of God. (Matthew 28:19)

RECONCILIATION is necessary for the forgiveness of sins. We confess our sins to a priest, as he represents Christ in the His church. For when we sin, we not only rupture our relationship with God, but also with our eternal community. Reconciliation heals these wounds and reunites us to Christ and our universal church. (John 20:21-23)

EUCHARIST completes our Christian initiation and serves as our spiritual nourishment. It is in receiving the Body and Blood of Christ that we unite ourselves to Christ. In response, we offer thanksgiving for God's protection and blessings. (Luke 22:19)

CONFIRMATION is necessary for the completion of our baptismal graces. It strengthens the baptized person, enabling him to witness to Christ effectively. As with Baptism, the Confirmand receives another indelible mark, marking one's total commitment to Christ. (Acts 8:14-16a, 17)

MARRIAGE provides the couple with God's grace to commit to a lifelong relationship with each other. It unites the couple to Christ indissolubly. The spouse's love for each other bears witness to God's irrevocable love for us, as they remain open to new life. (Mark 10:6-9)

HOLY ORDERS provide the newly ordained with God's grace to live up to their commitment to serve God. At ordination, priests receive a sacred power to lead, teach and sanctify the faithful. As with Baptism and Confirmation, those receiving the sacrament of Holy Orders obtain an indelible mark on their souls, marking them as servants of Christ. (Deacon: 1 Timothy 3:8-10, 12-13) (Priest: Acts 14:23) (Bishop: Titus 1:7-9)

ANOINTING OF THE SICK provides the infirmed with God's strength, peace and courage, reducing any anxiety over death. Within this sacrament, the infirm also partakes in the sacraments of Reconciliation and Eucharist to strengthen them for the journey from this life to the next. (James 5:14-15)

Chapter 9 Study Guide
Handing on Our Faith-Filled Gifts

In chapter 9, we discussed the *foundation of faith*, specifically the sacraments. We examined the importance of handing on these faith-filled gifts to the next generation. We recognized the value of the sacraments in forming the moral conscience of our children. We discussed how these moral principles are foundational in all cradle Catholics who share in the sacraments, even if they are not consciously aware of it. Let's challenge ourselves to become more competent and intentional in understanding the value of our foundation of faith in our daily lives.

- How can fathers make themselves more available to sharing their faith and explaining the importance of the sacraments to their children and families with intent?

- How do the sacraments form a foundation of faith that cascades throughout all aspects of our lives?

- Which sacraments have I and my family members received? What have I observed in the way these sacraments have strengthened my own family?

- How does the Holy Spirit work through me and my family as we celebrate the Mass together? Do we approach Communion with full intent and with an awareness of what we are about to receive?

- How does the sacrament of Reconciliation help us to share fully in all the other sacraments? Do I, as the spiritual head and protector of my family, make sure that I, and my family, receive this sacrament regularly?

- What examples can we share from our own families (or others) of how the foundation of faith has provided children with the moral conviction necessary to make good decisions in difficult circumstances?

- How have the lives of intentional parents, who hand on their faith-filled gifts, been somewhat shielded from the emotional upheavals that inevitably challenge all families?

- How has God's grace provided a clarity of truth that helped me, or my family, through a challenge that would have been difficult to overcome otherwise?

- Can we become competent to the commitment and composure needed daily to reflect the moral posture required to successfully nurture a faith-filled family?

Handing on our faith-filled gifts has never been more important than here and now. We now live in a culture where the elite ruling class, and majority of entertainment and media, try intentionally to dismiss the Christian faith and the traditions that go with it. We live in a society that trades traditions for trends.

The society that my generation grew up in still largely values morality. My parent's generation could be somewhat unintentional in their parenting, and still trust that their children would understand right and wrong. They envisioned their children would "eventually get it" by the time they reached adulthood. This stance was a reasonable one for them to assume because society at large shared a common sense of morality and family values. My siblings and I are better off for the intentional faith-filled family that our parents shared with us. But even for the cradle Catholic of my time, who did not have intentional faith-filled parents, the foundation of faith instilled in them through the sacraments remained steady. This occurred only because we had the cooperation of a morally upright society that transcended from generations that supported family values and faith traditions.

Today's generation of parents, however, must work harder. For this and future generations, the foundation of faith will only be built upon, and through, intentional parents. Without recognizing the value of the sacraments, and how they support, form, and cascade into all aspects of our lives, future generations will lose the faith that leads to God's Grace. Fathers, become aware of this fact. Take your rightful place as the spiritual head of your family. Take care in handing on your faith-filled gifts to the families you nurture. Intentionally practice your faith. Grow in your faith. Help build your family's foundation of faith in the New Covenant and the sacraments, and you will lead your family into a peaceful worldly existence. You, too, can share in the satisfaction of handing on, in love, what love has made.

Notes:

_____

_____

_____

_____

_____

_____

_____

_____

_____

_____

_____

_____

_____

_____

_____

Chapter 10
Conscious Competence

*Raymond, you do not have to listen to me, but you are going to
have to hear me.*
~ *Blanche Fanelli (My Grandmother)*

Let's explore the concept of unconscious competence. After introducing this concept, we will explore the principles behind it. We will focus primarily on the third step, conscious competence. It is in this step where we find ourselves becoming intentional in what we strive to achieve.

Becoming unconsciously competent as an intentional father will strengthen all areas of our lives, but most importantly the way we approach the growth of our children and families. I believe this awareness provides a clear perspective of the composure and compassion needed for an intentional father to introduce a new task or life lesson to his children. As any parent knows, children learn through repetition, and mastery of a new task or skill requires lots of repetition. It is easy for us to become frustrated when we try to lead without seeing immediate results. Understanding unconscious competence will enable us to practice the virtue of temperance when approaching life lessons and sharing needed competencies within the families we nurture.

The concept focuses on key factors that affect our thinking as we learn new skills: consciousness or awareness, and the achievement of competence. Let's look at how we move through the different stages of competence.[7]

1. **Unconscious Incompetence** – We are not aware of the skill or that it needs to be learned.

2. **Conscious Incompetence** – The skill has been introduced, and we begin to work on it.

3. **Conscious Competence** – We have acquired the skill at a basic level but have not yet mastered it to the point of unconscious competence.

4. **Unconscious competence** – We have practiced the skill, or task, for a period, and it has now become an unconscious competence. In other words, we achieved competence in this skill, or task, to the point that it becomes second nature to us.

The first step of **unconscious incompetence** is where some people/fathers, who have expectations of others/children, can become confused. Just because we have a certain skill or competency does not mean that others share the same skill or competency. To provide a very basic example, just because a father understands the importance of washing his hands before dinner does not mean that his child will automatically be aware of and choose to practice the same task. Moving from becoming aware or conscious of a task, to developing an understanding of its value, to turning it into a lifelong good habit takes time and repetition. Fathers who take time out to recognize this and to share their knowledge of the task that is expected, will help alleviate unnecessary confusion over time.

In the second step of **conscious incompetence**, a new task is introduced. This step is not as simple as it might first appear. As fathers, *how* we choose to introduce a new task or skill, to our children and the families we nurture is very important. Do we dictate? Or, do we demonstrate? Do we fail to introduce the new task or skill at all? For example, as fathers, we must introduce our faith in God to our children. If we, as parents, fail to even *introduce* this important and foundational piece of knowledge, how will our children's lives and spirituality be affected as a result? Intentional fathers will introduce a new task, skill, or concept in a way that inspires their families to want to develop it further and master it over time.

Now we move to the third step, **conscious competence** the most critical step in the learning process. We need to be fully intentional, practicing composure in either learning or sharing a task, or skill with our families to avoid setbacks in the process.

It generally takes adults three weeks to move from the second step of conscious incompetence, to full awareness in the fourth step of **unconscious competence** for a newly introduced task or skill to be mastered. If three weeks is typical for an adult to move through the stages, then how long might it take a child to do so?

We need to keep the level of consciousness in mind as we approach teaching new skills to our children. With knowledge, we can understand our responsibility as fathers to practice composure and repetitively share a task in which our children need to grow. Understanding the need for encouragement and repetition will alleviate frustration as we accept this as a known competency. Applying this concept in all other aspects of our lives will greatly benefit our own personal journeys as well.

While I was a little boy living across the street from my grandparents, I learned many life lessons from them. During my adolescent years, my grandmother would always lead into a lesson with: "Raymond, you do not have to listen to me, but you are going to have to hear me." There is tremendous wisdom in that statement. Those words acted as a subconscious "switch" that silently turned on my attention to something important I was about to hear. The lessons my grandmother intentionally and repetitively shared with me rang true throughout my life.

I heard those words many times in my head. I, too, found value in using her words to lead into the lessons I shared with my sons, especially during their adolescent years. I believe that my intent and my repetitive use of this expression when they were young turned on that silent, subconscious switch to the importance of the lesson about to be shared for them as well. I can only hope that the lessons I shared with my sons will remain in their thoughts and ring true throughout their lives. Repetition is how we all learn in all aspects of life.

Chapter 10 Study Guide
Conscious Competence

In chapter 10, we discussed the concept of *unconscious competence*. We became competent to the four steps within the process that help us achieve unconscious competence. We especially focused on the third step, *conscious competence*, and showed how it can help alleviate a father's feelings of frustration over repeating the same task or lesson over and over, while seeing no immediate results. This concept sheds light on the fact that repetition is essential to the learning process.

For our children to grow in knowledge and achieve a level of unconscious competence in any given task or skill, they must be guided by intentional fathers who demonstrate composure and compassion as they repeat life lessons over time. This concept is an important tool to help intentional fathers develop a clear perspective and reasonable expectations as they fulfill their obligation of leading and nurturing their families' growth.

- What is the concept of unconscious competence? How does it serve as a tool for helping fathers share lessons with the families they nurture?

- What is an example from my own life of how I achieved unconscious competence in an important skill or life lesson? Can I see how I followed the stages to reach mastery of that skill or life lesson?

- Did my father use this tool, and if so, how? How might I use my past experiences with my father to move forward in the way that I father my children?

- Why are the disciplines of composure and compassion so important to the intentional father who shares a new task with his children? How have I modeled (or failed to model) these disciplines in my own family relationships?

- How can personal frustration and the desire for immediate gratification impede the process of helping our children attain the level of unconscious competence for a given skill or task?

- How can this concept benefit us as we work each day to face our own challenges and chip away at the wedges that keep us from growing in knowledge and faith?

The concept of unconscious competence can lend truth to the fact that any bad habit can be broken generally within the same period that it would take to learn a good habit. I do not suggest this is true for physical dependencies like addictions, but I say that we can use this concept to improve ourselves. For example, if you find yourself using God's name in vain, then by intentionally practicing not to do this for a period of time, (approximately three weeks) you will eventually no longer use God's name in vain. You will overcome that bad habit. This is just one example of how we can continue to introduce and master new life lessons within our adult lives as we become more competent at using our willpower to conquer the hurdles we face.

Notes:

_____

_____

_____

_____

_____

_____

_____

_____

_____

_____

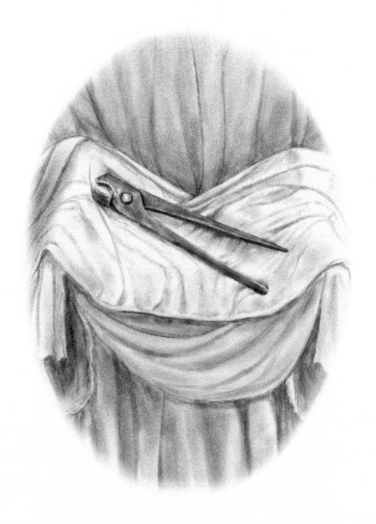

Chapter 11
Juggling Life

Just as in a successful marriage, it is necessary to find the fluid motion that works by learning how to dance together peacefully through life. Learning how to juggle life gracefully is where we will find ourselves achieving peace of mind...

Early in my career I was introduced to a concept, or tool, designed to help managers become more compassionate toward their employees' needs. This concept helps managers and employees achieve a healthier work/life balance. The concept illustrated five balls of life that everyone must juggle. The balls were described as: faith, family, health, friendship, and work. In the management scenario presented to me, the family ball was made of glass, and all the rest were made of rubber. This exercise shed light on the importance of family, and how, if the family ball were to be dropped, it could shatter to pieces. This exercise also gave me an awareness and foundation for understanding the importance of juggling various elements of life. The exercise stresses that a reasonable expectation is to be able to juggle only three balls in the air at any given time. Further, it points to the importance of choosing the right three balls to juggle each day. There are now many sources on the internet that address this concept. Let me share my thoughts with you on this topic as I apply it to the foundation of faith, yet in a different context.

Let's look at the balls to be juggled as having moral characteristics rather than aspects, or facets, of our lives. Let's consider them not as the "five balls of life," but rather as the "five balls of morality." We can intentionally apply this concept in our daily lives while attempting to master our morality, ever conscious of our flawed humanity. This will demonstrate clearly the virtues needed while attempting to juggle life with moral posture in mind and how to become successful in the act.

Let's start with the *faith* ball. This ball is made of our soul and will be known as the ball of truth. The faith ball shares with us what is true and real through God's grace, which guides us without fail throughout our life journey.

The next ball is *family*. It represents our will and our foundation in life. I agree that if dropped, the family ball could shatter irreparably. It is within the family that we find our will and an understanding of the importance of handing on our faith-filled gifts within the families we nurture.

The third ball is *health*. This ball is made up of time and represents our mortality and our center in life. This ball makes clear to us the worth of the balls we choose to juggle at any given time and adds value to the balance needed to continue juggling well.

The fourth ball is *friendship*. This ball is where we find our selflessness. We must recognize that our basic instinct, within our sinful human nature, is to hurt each other. Understanding and becoming aware of this fact and learning to accept and love each other past our faults is what leads to the selflessness needed to successfully juggle this ball. Envision that there are many friendship balls to choose from, and that another juggler must throw their ball to you to be able to put their ball into play. If you don't find the friendship ball you are looking to receive being available to you during active play, then accept letting that ball go. Learning how to receive a well-handled friendship ball into the act of juggling will add to the fluid motion needed to perfect the overall act. It may require dropping a few of these balls before becoming proficient at juggling the friendship ball. This ball adds balance and stamina needed to master the art of juggling the remaining morality balls.

The final ball is *work*. This ball is made up of our integrity. At work we do not get to surround ourselves with like-minded people. We get exposed to many different views and opinions, we get judged, and we judge others. The influence of the chaotic world is most prevalent in our work lives. Our integrity – the ability to discern right from wrong, and to choose the right – is an important characteristic to guide us throughout our careers. Our integrity graces us with an awareness of the need to chip away at our sinful and selfish nature while we are at work. We should keep in mind that abrasive relationships can serve us well because they help us practice composure and self-discipline. Such difficult relationships act like sandpaper, smoothing out our rough edges as we learn and grow.

Let's review. The five balls of morality:

- Faith = our soul

- Family = our will

- Health = our mortality

- Friendship = our selflessness

- Work = our integrity

Now that we have the concept down, we can gain clarity for considering which three balls we should juggle at any given time. Make a mental note that there are two morality balls that should never be at rest within the concept of juggling life. The *faith* and *family* balls should be viewed as primary. These balls should always be in the air. The concept of creating balance in our life comes when we decide which one of the three remaining morality balls we introduce into the act while juggling the two primary balls. If we consciously or unconsciously choose to leave out one of the two primary balls, then we will find ourselves off-center and out of balance. Why is this?

If we lose focus, or lose our grip, on the importance of properly handling our faith and family within the act of juggling life, then we more easily submit to temptations. We fall short within our sinful nature, while juggling all the demands of living in our physical world.

To juggle the five balls of morality successfully, we must work at finding our own fluid motion. Working at perfecting the technique according to our abilities, while accepting our own limitations in the process, will help us find our balance. Just as in a successful marriage, it is necessary to find the fluid motion that works by learning how to dance together peacefully through life. Learning how to juggle life gracefully is where we will find ourselves achieving peace of mind. By having realistic expectations and knowing that some form of failure is inevitable, we will find that failure will help us to grow while we refine the process.

Each challenge in life prepares us for the next. The way we approach these challenges reveals our integrity and our character to the world around us. This holds true when we choose to make fair and honorable decisions. Thus, the process of making difficult choices becomes less difficult because of our history of fair-mindedness that built our character and informed our decision-making process. Becoming conscious of the need for maintaining balance, while juggling all the morality balls within our chaotic world, will add immeasurable value to all aspects of our lives. Over time we will be able to naturally trust our choice of balls to juggle, and we will be able to keep them in the air without even having to look at them. Finding center and balance through the act of juggling the demands of life will become an unconscious competence in good time.

So how do we find center and balance in life? There is no easy answer, but I believe that three factors are essential: spiritual, mental, and physical health and well-being. All these factors, together, will help us achieve the healthy balance and centering we desire. If any one of these is absent, we find ourselves off-center, leading to feelings of weariness or restlessness.

If we are not aware of the importance of spirituality in finding our center, then we may not ever recognize the reason(s) why we are restless and feel off-center. In life, we can never have total control over any situation. However, we can intentionally place order into every situation we face. An awareness that change is inevitable, and usually out of our control, needs to be part of the equation always. Setting realistic expectations, and knowing our limitations, will help us form healthy habits for juggling the morality balls of life.

A word of caution here. Become mindful of the ball that you take for granted; it is usually the most important ball in the air. Within the actual act of juggling, we can feel frustrated when we fail or fumble, but we must remain strong in our commitment to learn from our mistakes and keep moving forward. One day, when we become expert jugglers and make it all look so easy, we will look back and find it hard to imagine the time when we were unable to juggle at all.

Chapter 11 Study Guide
Juggling Life

In chapter 11 we explored the concept of juggling life. We became competent to the theory of juggling life's balls: faith, family, health, friendship, and work. We expanded and built off that theory to view the juggled balls as five balls of morality: Faith = our soul, Family = our will, Health = our mortality, Friendship = our selflessness, Work = our integrity. We noted that the primary balls of *faith* and *family* always need to be in the air to support and give clarity to the third ball we choose to juggle at any given time. We became aware of the need for finding our center through the balance we gain from our spiritual, mental, and physical well-being. We discussed how being consistent at making fair and honorable decisions makes future difficult decisions seem easy through the character gained.

Let's consider how we can apply these concepts to our personal lives.

- How do the five juggling balls represent my own morality? Take time to contemplate how you've experienced each in your life to date.

- Why are the faith and family balls considered primary among the five? Provide examples of how they interact with, and support, the three remaining balls.

- What happens if we drop the family and/or the faith ball? If dropped, is the damage always irreparable?

- What does the friendship ball teach us about practice making perfect the true nature of the friendship ball? Why must we learn to "let go," if we do not receive the ball we are looking to juggle?

- Why is the work ball one of the most difficult ones to juggle? What happens if we let our guard down with this ball?

- What three elements of health help us achieve balance and center as we juggle life's demands? If we cultivate these elements well, what benefits will they achieve for the families we nurture?

- Why do some people fail to recognize that they are off center or restless? What enables people to experience healthy growth?

- How does a pattern of poor decision-making cascade into every aspect of our lives? What happens, over time, if we commit to fairness and honor in our decision-making as we juggle life's demands?

Finding balance and making good decisions are two key elements needed in the act of juggling life. The morality balls that we juggle will remain in fluid motion if we observe these key elements, along with one other: communication. As a people, communication is both our greatest achievement and our most profound failure. We have various forms of communication – mail, telephone, radio, film, television – and in recent times, social media, such as Facebook, Twitter, and Snapchat. Snapchat allows our children to create snippets of communication that last for only a brief moment of time (What does this approach promote?). Yet, with all this technology and numerous ways to connect, we find great difficulty in communicating one-on one. When we come face to face with each other, our words do not match our body language. We hold back for fear of what our realness might reveal. We find it safer to be untruthful, whether consciously or subconsciously, rather than share a truth that might be painful. And our culture accepts – even expects – this sad reality. Consider how we accept repeated lies by the politicians that we continually vote back into office.

Look back over the generations and consider what our chosen leaders have taught our children as socially acceptable. Does truth even have a place in our society anymore? How many variations of the perception of truth are there? Are we at a point where we make up our own situational truths through our own free will and believe wholeheartedly in what we perpetuate? These questions reflect the constant doubt from which we cannot escape while living in the physical world.

Choosing to seek out and communicate absolute truth, with good intent, should become a competency within our moral character. Truth, even a hurtful truth, shared without malice, ultimately leads to healthy growth. Understanding this fact and always being truthful with the family we nurture will instill virtues that will cascade into every aspect of our family's lives.

Intentional thoughts lead to actions. Intentional actions lead to habits. Intentional habits lead to an unconscious competence reflecting true moral posture to all who come in contact with the intentional man who juggles life's morality balls well.

Notes:

_____

_____

_____

_____

_____

_____

_____

_____

_____

_____

Chapter 12
A Faithful Mindset

Through the truth shared within moments of grace, we gain knowledge to stop listening to the subconscious voices that keep whispering to us that we are not good enough for God's grace to be revealed in our lives...

We realize a faithful mindset through daily reflection, with a demeanor of humility and compassion throughout the intentional journey, within the arch of life. We willfully accept God's unconditional love and forgiveness through the sacrament of Reconciliation. When we approach this sacrament with humility and a genuine sorrow for our sins, in true contrition, God showers His grace upon us. This provides clarity of truth about His love, empowering us with a strong desire to avoid sin. We begin to find our worth within our Father's eyes, and we gain the strength needed to chip away at our sinful nature and the vices/wedges that cling to our daily lives.

Humility is such an important catalyst for our capacity to receive God's grace and develop a faithful mindset. Let's consider, for a moment, the role that humility plays.

Humility is associated with the cardinal virtue of temperance because temperance includes all the virtues that restrain or express the inordinate movements of our desires or appetites. Therefore, humility serves as a check on our egos, refraining us from boasting about our accomplishments.

Catholic.com[8] offers several definitions on the virtue of humility:

- a quality by which a person considering his own defects has a humble opinion of himself and willingly submits himself to God and to others for God's sake.

- a virtue by which a man knowing himself as he truly is, abases himself. Jesus Christ is the ultimate definition of Humility. (St. Bernard of Clairvaux)

- a virtue that consists in keeping oneself within one's own bounds, not reaching out to things above one, but submitting to God (St. Thomas Aquinas).

Humility leads us to the sacrament of Reconciliation. Through truth, we share in moments of grace received in this sacrament. We gain the knowledge to stop listening to the subconscious voices that keep whispering to us that we are not good enough for God's grace to be revealed in our lives. Recognize moments of grace. Do not dismiss them. For these moments are the building blocks in our foundation of faith that enable us to chip away at the layers of sin within our daily lives.

It is through understanding the power of our free will that we gain the strength needed to choose to act rightly. We become knowledgeable of the power of Reconciliation as an important channel of grace. It is here where we are made clean and restored in perfect unity with our heavenly Father.

Our faithfulness is revealed through our actions and our commitment to truly want to sin no more. Our will takes hold of our lives as we share in the truth that is revealed while we are in God's grace. As we move forward intentionally in our faith journey, we understand that nothing can make us worthless in God's eyes. We learn to live our lives through the lessons learned in moments of grace. We apply these lessons with love and compassion.

I was not always intentional with my faith. I did, at one time not so long ago, practice a rote faith. My first step in my arch of life journey in the Catholic Church started in my mid-40s. My oldest son Nicholas informed me that I was not understanding my foundation of faith built within the sacraments of the New Covenant.

I was living a rote faith, unaware of the fullness of truth found within our Church. I now recognize that my foundation of faith was always within me thanks to my sacramental life in the New Covenant. I also recognize how easy it is to practice a rote Catholic faith. My understanding of the Mass lends clarity to this reality. The repetitiveness of the Mass combined with my lack of understanding of the meaning of the parts of the Mass, contributed to my practicing a rote faith. I experienced the Mass as an obligation. This world leads us all to believe that everything is about us. We, therefore, seek out congregations that cater to our humanity and our desire for entertainment and recognition. Understanding the Mass as a sacrificial offering to God leads to a clearer perspective of its importance, strengthened through the mystery of faith in the sacrament of the Eucharist. Jesus, Himself, handed down to us this Mystery of Faith at the Last Supper; the first Mass.

For a long time, I felt a responsibility to share these truths with other Catholic men as well as all men of faith. As a Catholic, sharing my faith can be difficult because of the negative judgments that have been cast upon the Church at this moment in time. However, these judgments are born through the bias and sinful nature of man-made ideals and issues. I came to realize that they hold no truth within the Church's history. The truth of our Church goes back to the gift handed on from Jesus Himself before all our worldly sin could shadow Her. Seek and find truth in what is real. Do not submit to creating your own version of what the Church should look like by lending value to a worldly cause that can separate you from sharing in God's grace. True faith is found in God, not in man.

We are all truly God's children. It is through prejudice that faithful men find themselves divided. Bias is a learned behavior that helps to confuse many of the faithful. Bias and prejudice toward any of God's children originates from our sinful nature. Although we are all born within the state of original sin, it is through faith that God's grace leads us to unity. We can strive to rise above our sinful nature and love one another as our heavenly Father loves His Church. If you can become aware of the need for God's grace in your life, you will need little effort in finding a faithful mindset within your personal journey of owning your own faith.

God's grace, and the means in which we obtain and share in grace, is what so many of us are searching so desperately for to make us feel whole. Recognize this and work actively, and intentionally, toward receiving God's grace. Become aware of the fact that God's grace can easily be masked by our will to submit to a cause. Become knowledgeable of the fact that our confusion is due to our acceptance of false or situational truths that lead us to wander aimlessly, unaware that we are separating ourselves from God's grace.

As people, we all want someone to look to for guidance. This is true in all aspects of life. How many employees respect the manager who does not give them direction? This holds true in our families as well.

As fathers, responsible for the spiritual and physical well-being of our families, we have one true source for guidance - our heavenly Father, whose teachings reveal the humility required to nurture our families. Our words and actions can cut deeper than any physical scar. Recognize and own this fact. We must love ourselves before we can love others. We all need to take a good look at ourselves and form a humble opinion. We need to recognize the work needed, within our own health and well-being, to reflect love and compassion toward our family as God intends. Chipping away at life's sinful nature requires us to look within our own lives and accept the challenges we personally need to address.

What is key to understand is that we need to address the flaws in our own character before we can do any good for our family. When we recognize our sinful nature and practice temperance to chip away at the vices that seek to entrap us, we will find our worth as children of God. As fathers, our guidance comes from our Heavenly Father's teachings and grace. With His strength and fortitude, as well as ownership of our own free will, we will continue to grow in a faithful mindset.

Chapter 12 Study Guide
A Faithful Mindset

In chapter 12, we discussed the importance of a faithful mindset in our daily lives. We achieve that faithful mindset through daily reflection with a demeanor of humility and compassion, as we move forward on our intentional journey throughout the arch of life. We discussed how our first step in this journey is through the acceptance that our heavenly Father loves us and forgives our sins unconditionally, as we confess our sins with true contrition and remorse. We considered how we, as fathers, must also unconditionally forgive our own children. Let's discuss some ways in which we can develop a faithful mindset:

- What is a demeanor of humility and compassion? How does it support a healthy and faithful mindset?

- Why is it hard to accept that God unconditionally loves us and forgives us our sins?

- How is God's grace the answer for what so many souls desperately search for but do not recognize due to the confusion of living in and of this world?

- How does the sacrament of Reconciliation serve as a channel by which God's mercy can dispel our misery?

- What is revealed to us when we are in God's grace?

- How do we find the strength to forgive others as God forgives us?

- How does regularly receiving the sacrament of Reconciliation help us to form a desire to sin no more and to intentionally chip away at the layers of sin in our daily lives?

- Who gave us the Church? How does our knowledge of this historical truth affect the way we interpret how the world tries to define the Church?

- What can separate us from God's grace? What can separate people of faith from each other?

- How does our willpower aid us in rising above our sinful nature and loving all of God's children as God loves His people?

- Who is a father's best source of guidance? How does a faithful mindset create peace of mind within ourselves and within the families we nurture?

Unless we have humility, we cannot say we are sorry. Consider it a strength to say that you are sorry as your faults present themselves. It is one of the most important lessons we can share with our families. Through our humility, we teach virtuous lessons to the families we nurture that cascade into their foundation of faith throughout their lives. Recognizing a faithful mindset is one of the most important lessons we can reflect into the lives of the families we nurture

Notes:

_____

_____

_____

_____

_____

_____

_____

_____

_____

_____

_____

_____

_____

_____

_____

_____

Chapter 13
God's Grace in the Faith-Filled Family

*We receive moments of grace, during our first efforts toward
owning our own faith; moments that share with us what is true
and real. There are no coincidences when we intentionally
pursue our faith journey...*

God presents the faith-filled family to mankind as a gift through
His son Jesus, within the blood of the New Covenant, and the graces
bestowed in the sacramental life. Searching for what is true and real
will always lead back to the Body of Christ, our One, Holy, Catholic,
and Apostolic Church. However, some cradle Catholics do not value
the Church because they do not understand it. Because they are blind
to its source and purpose, they are quick to find fault in the Church or
to dismiss it as antiquated or irrelevant. I believe that some of these
same cradle Catholics long for the truth and genuinely want to
experience the clarity it brings, but they have no idea how to find it.
In addition, we live in a spoon-fed society, hungry for instant
gratification, which supports the mindset that we should be given
everything we want, without effort.

Our faith is ours to own. Yet, it requires effort to sustain – an
effort fueled by our own free will. Even a minimal effort on our part
to chip away at the layers of sin will stimulate the strength needed to
endure living in and of this world. We receive moments of grace,
during our first efforts toward owning our own faith; moments that
share what is true and real in our hearts and will. We must recognize
these moments and not dismiss them, I call them "God-incidents."
There are no coincidences when we intentionally pursue our faith
journey. The moments of grace we experience provide the strength we
need to endure the worldly view as a faithful witness.

When was the last time you thought about your soul, or even
heard the word spoken aloud? Maybe when you heard a priest say,
"The souls of the faithfully departed," during Mass? Will you share in

a faith that ultimately leads you to be one of the "faithfully departed"? Do you ever think about "eternal rest" being granted unto you?

The world around us does not encourage or support such a mindset. The world attempts to shake our faith to the core by its constant attacks on the Catholic Church. It hopes these attacks will completely fracture the foundation of faith that sustains our lives and discourage us from looking beyond the moment we are in toward what is eternal. The battles against the Body of Christ, the Church, are intentional. We need to become aware of this reality. Today, the Church may be perceived as weak or corrupt in the minds of men, but we must remember the Church is not a finite part of a specific moment in time. The Church is universal and eternal (universal is the definition of the word Catholic)! Its chief work is to promote the eternal salvation of mankind. Become aware of this fact and find the amazing value of owning your own faith. Your faith is the "pearl of great price" that helps you build a foundation of faith within the family you nurture – an eternal faith grounded in the truth of the New Covenant and the sacraments shared in the apostolic teachings of our universal Church.

Doubt and apathy are two stumbling blocks that the world casts before us. If we constantly doubt the truth of the Church or we do not care to seek the truth, then we allow ourselves to be duped. Think for yourself. Use your intellectual curiosity to identify objective truth that defines your concept of faith and the Church. My oldest son says it best:

> *The Church is great because She has all the answers,*
> *but challenging because to find them you have to seek*
> *them out for yourself.*

There is a lot of truth in that statement for cradle Catholics who have opted to live in the moment, in and of this world, who have not intentionally invested in their faith since their childhood lessons beyond attending Mass. The Mass is not about us. It is a holy sacrifice offered up to God at His command, where we all share in the bread of life, the Eucharist, which keeps us in union (communion) with the Holy Spirit. It is not meant to be about us. Understanding this fact will prevent us from practicing a rote faith. A faithful search for the truth will lead us to an eternal rest, with the added benefit of learning how to live peacefully in the physical world. God sees our effort! We cannot outdo God's compassion and mercy. Anything is possible, when we live in God's grace.

Let's venture through Scripture to highlight some of the people and events that have contributed to the God-given gifts of the Body of Christ, our Church. The continuity of - God's chosen people - as well as the celebration and sacrifice of the Mass will be our focal point.

This chapter will outline undeniable facts that span from the Old Testament (the first five covenants) through this moment in time. I hope this quick review ignites your heart, sparks your intellectual curiosity, and clarifies any worldly confusion that has been cast upon His One, Holy, Catholic, and Apostolic Church. I encourage each of you to expand your own knowledge of the history of the covenants and the sacraments by reading Holy Scripture to find what is true and good and beautiful about the apostolic teachings of our Church.

To impart God's grace, He entered into five Old Testament covenants between Himself and man. We define covenant as a sacred promise between family members. The covenants that God made with mankind (His beloved sons and daughters) were mediated through the following individuals: Adam, Noah, Abraham, Moses, David, (Old Testament) and finally, Jesus Christ (New Testament), who continues to mediate the covenant that we all share in union with Him today. Let's focus briefly on three of the covenants; those with Abraham, Moses, and David, and on the fulfillment of all the covenants through Jesus Christ. These Old Testament covenants offer some clarity on who we truly are as God's chosen people in the sixth and final covenant, with Jesus Christ.

Abraham

In reward for Abraham's faithfulness and obedience, God promises Abraham that he will have as many descendants as there are stars in the sky. From Abraham's grandson Jacob, also known as Israel, came the 12 tribes of Israel - the Israelites — (later known as the "Jews" or followers of Judaism). The Israelites were called God's chosen people.

Moses

Moses, a descendant of the tribe of Levi, led the Israelites out of Egypt during the Exodus. On Mount Sinai, God gave Moses the Ten Commandments, which we know as the Mosaic Law or the Mosaic Covenant. If the Israelites would remain faithful to the Mosaic Covenant, then God promised they would become a great nation and be recognized throughout the world as His chosen people. Within the Mosaic covenant, animal sacrifices were offered in a tabernacle, or tent-sanctuary, in the desert. These animals symbolized the false gods of the Egyptians and served as a foreshadowing of the true sacrificial offering that would be made by the true God in the Messianic age to come. Sadly, the Israelites failed to remain faithful to the covenant. They turned away from God and fashioned and worshiped a golden calf. But God did not give up on His people.

David

After the Israelites entered the Promised Land and set up a kingdom for themselves, God made a covenant with young David, the second king of Israel and a descendant of the tribe of Judah. God promised David that his heirs would become kings over all the earth and would be known as sons of God and would build the house of God. As promised, King David's son, Solomon, built the Temple, which contained the holy sanctuary where the presence of God dwelt among His people, with an outer courtyard with an altar where all sacrificial offerings were performed. But again, the people failed to keep God's covenant. The Temple was destroyed by King Nebuchadnezzar of Babylon and lay in ruins for more than 50 years until the Babylonian exile ended. King Cyrus of Persia, anointed by God, permitted the Jews to return to Jerusalem to rebuild their Temple.

Jesus Christ, sixth and final covenant

After the Temple was rebuilt, the Jews, particularly a sect called the Pharisees, again perverted the Mosaic covenant through their hypocrisy and worldly interpretation of God's law. Again, God did not give up on His people. God sent the greatest mediator of all – His only son, Jesus, to save the world. At 30 years old, Jesus Himself shared in the sacrament of Baptism. He who is without sin allowed Himself to be baptized by St. John the Baptist to show all God's children how to follow Him into the New Covenant.

Jesus began His public ministry at the wedding feast of Cana, where He witnessed the sacrament of Matrimony. Over the next three years, Jesus prepared God's children for the New Covenant. Knowing that soon He must return to the Father, Jesus established His Church upon the Rock of St. Peter and promised that no one would have the power to destroy His Church. Jesus said to His disciple Simon, "Thou art Peter and upon this rock I will build my Church and the gates of hell shall not prevail against it, and I will give to thee the keys to the kingdom of heaven and whatsoever thou shall bind upon earth, it shall be bound also in heaven. And whatsoever thou loose upon earth, it shall be loosed also in heaven" (Mt 16:18-19).

Through St. Peter, our first pope, and all popes who followed him in apostolic succession, Jesus grants the divine guidance to do the Father's will, on earth, as it is in heaven. He helps those who will listen to understand that anyone who accepts Christ in their heart, as the true Son of God will become part of the New Israel - God's chosen people - whether Gentile or Jew. At the Last Supper, Jesus completed His public ministry, and established the Body of Christ, His Church, by sharing the sacrament of First Communion, celebrating the first Mass.

The Jewish high priests, however, did not accept the authority of Jesus or His apostles. The Jewish authorities were living in and of this world. They did not want to lose their worldly power. In one of His parables (cf. Mk 12:1-12), Jesus asked the Jews what would become of the vineyard workers who killed the master's servants and then the master's son to keep the son's inheritance for themselves. Jesus said that the master would return and give the vineyard (the Kingdom of God) to others (that is, those who do the Father's will even if they are not Jews). The Jews were horrified by Jesus' words. Within this parable we see a foreshadowing of the New Covenant, which would be ushered in for all God's children, defined as those who follow the will of the Father.

After Jesus' Death, Resurrection, and Ascension, the Temple rebuilt by the Jews was destroyed in approximately 70 A.D., as foreshadowed in the Gospels where Jesus declared "not a stone upon a stone" (cf. Mt 24:2) would be left of the Temple. God would no longer dwell among His people within a man-made structure. Through the New Covenant, God would dwell within the hearts of His people; those who follow His Son. This truth is affirmed through Jesus' declaration that no one goes to the Father without going through the Son. Jesus, who is the fulfillment of the Old Covenant and who is the New Temple, hands on the New Covenant, achieved through His Passion, Death, and Resurrection, to His faithful followers through the saving work of His One, Holy, Catholic, and Apostolic Church.

It is within the Catholic Church that the greatest sacrifice of all is re-presented on the altar during the Mass. The re-presentation is the sole reason, and culminating factor, for the celebration of Mass. Through the mystery of faith, our offerings of bread and wine are transubstantiated (changed) into the Body and Blood of Jesus Christ. It is in this moment of the holy Mass when the priest raises high the bread of life, that heaven and earth are joined together in the universal church. No further sacrifices are needed to fulfill the New Covenant. Jesus is the Temple of Sacrifice raised up on the third day in fulfillment of the scriptures. The Holy Eucharist, received in the holy sacrifice of the Mass, is the principal sacrament celebrated in the Church. It invites us to participate in a spirit of thanksgiving in the mystery of our salvation, made possible by the sacrificial death and resurrection of Jesus Christ.

Jesus Christ was sent to save us all through the New Covenant, which we now share with God, Our Father in heaven. The New Covenant is for all God's children of faith. Anyone who sincerely seeks the truth cannot deny this fact, revealed in the Bible through the Gospel teachings. The Gospels were written by the apostles St. Matthew and St. John and by St. Mark and St. Luke, disciples of Jesus and scribes for the apostles, St. Peter and St. Paul. Their writings were preserved via apostolic succession. The handing on of the teachings of the apostles enlighten mankind to spread the Word of God through the Holy Spirit directly to their successors. The teachings of the Catholic Church do not sway as a result of apostolic succession. The apostles interacted with Jesus, and were chosen by Jesus, to be the first priests of the New Covenant. All teachings of the Church can be traced back to Jesus through the apostles, whose priesthood was conferred by the hands of Jesus Himself after His resurrection.

All fathers should develop an understanding of the New Covenant as a gift handed on to us from our heavenly Father through the Holy Spirit and the sacrifice of His only begotten Son. As fathers, we should recognize and commit to the necessity of handing on our faith-filled gifts and the sacraments to the families we nurture. We must actively share with our families that all faiths, denominations, and sects are some form of division from the One, Holy, Catholic, and Apostolic Church. Such awareness provides the clarity needed to see the truth beyond the worldly views.

Rest easy in the truth revealed through God's grace. Truth is what leads to *sharing* in God's grace. Be intentional in offering prayers for the souls of the faithful who find themselves separated from the knowledge of God's gifts and the sacraments, but who still search for what is true and real. Come peacefully to the realization that we are all part of God's faith-filled family in the Universal Church. Through humility, we should always choose to love all of God's children no matter where they are within their own journey in the arch of life.

Chapter 13 Study Guide
God's Grace in a Faith-Filled Family

In chapter 13, we became aware of the fact that Jesus is the fulfillment of the Old Testament by His ultimate sacrifice of dying on the cross. In His selflessness, Jesus Christ handed on the New Covenant, and the sacraments, to His followers to bring the gift of eternal salvation to all mankind. Within the New Covenant, we come to understand that anyone who accepts and follows Jesus Christ becomes part of the New Israel, which is now and forever God's chosen people. To lead people to the gift of eternal salvation, Jesus established the Body of Christ, His Universal Church. It is the One, Holy, Catholic, and Apostolic Church, which Jesus handed on to St. Peter, our first pope. The Holy Spirit continues to lead Jesus' Church via a succession of popes. Through the Church, God gifts His people with faith and the sacraments needed to stay in union with Him on the path to salvation. The Mass, which is the primary sacramental celebration, re-presents the sacrifice of Christ on the cross and becomes for the faithful a sacrificial offering to God. If we as Catholics truly understand this, we cannot practice a borrowed rote faith.

Let's take a moment to consider how becoming knowledgeable to the truth of the Church makes us accountable to the families we nurture and challenges us to:

1. Live in the Word (and not of this world)

2. Own our own faith

3. Share in God's grace as we build faith-filled families

Questions

- Do we fully understand that anyone who searches for what is true and real will ultimately be led back to the One, Holy, Catholic, and Apostolic Church?

- Why do some cradle Catholics think the Mass should be about them? Why do they fail to see that the Mass is a sacrificial offering that Jesus asked His disciples to do intentionally in remembrance of Him?

- What does it say about our faith if we place more value in how the evening news depicts the Church than in how the Scripture describes the Church or how the Church works for the salvation of mankind? Do we place our faith in man or in God?

- How does studying Scripture strengthen our faith?

- How does the Parable of the Wicked Tenants in the Vineyard describe the fulfillment of the New Covenant?

- How is Jesus Christ a fulfillment of the Old Covenant and how did He usher in the New Covenant?

- Who were God's chosen people in the Old Covenant? Who are God's chosen people in the New Covenant?

- What did Jesus establish to ensure that mankind would find their way to the gift of eternal salvation? How does Peter and apostolic succession play a role in ensuring this gift will always be available to God's people?

- When was the first Mass? What did Jesus sacrifice for us at that time, and what sacrificial offering do we make in return today? How does the sacrament of Communion relate to the Mass? How does the sacrament of Reconciliation relate to the Mass?

- Who can destroy the One, Holy, Catholic, and Apostolic Church? How does Scripture support your answer?

- What does the authority of Jesus Christ and His apostles in the Church teach us about the authority of fathers in the home? Why are faith-filled families under attack by society?

- Where do we find evidence that the Church is intentionally and constantly under attack and portrayed as weak and corrupt, particularly at this moment in time? Is the Church a finite, temporal institution or an eternal gift of salvation from a loving Father? Explain how Holy Scripture and/or the apostolic teachings support your answer.

- What is the definition of eternal salvation? Who are the souls of the faithfully departed? What does it mean to rest in peace?

- As fathers, how can we become more intentional and competent in our understanding that the foundation of faith is forever built up and shared in God's grace through a faith-filled family?

- Do we understand the meaning of the Universal Church?

Strong families, who build a foundation of faith by following a clear moral compass, determine the ultimate strength of any society. As fathers, we need to continually grow in humility and selflessness, by exercising our free will according to the faith and moral teachings of the Church. Our commitment to such growth will provide strength and fortitude throughout our intentional faith journey.

Strength and fortitude will remove the wedges of sin firmly placed in our lives and help us to endure the challenges of living in and of this world. Faith leads to God's grace. Sharing in God's grace will make clear to us what is true and real. It will provide the foundation of faith needed to love our families as Christ loves His Church and will ultimately instill God's grace in the faith-filled family.

Remember, before we can lead, we must first follow. Our moral compass will be our guide, as we consciously commit to intentionally and faithfully leading our families daily by following the teachings of the New Covenant and sharing in the gifts of grace found in the sacraments. When we intentionally stay on the path, our reward will be twofold. We and our families receive peace of mind and ultimately, salvation and eternal rest for a life well lived as a good and worthy servant. This is true for all who seek out and share in the faith that leads to God's grace in the arch of life.

Make a conscious effort to always look to good men for guidance, as you focus on the composure and commitment needed to fight the good fight throughout your masculine journey. The truth shared in God's grace will allow you to see clearly as you rise above the sinful nature of your humanity, while living in, but not of, this world. Commit to holding yourself and other like-minded men accountable on your journey by sharing in the Word in men's groups. This will aid in strengthening and building up moral family values and the needed sense of community that our children and society are so desperately missing. The good choices men make will reflect well on the families they lead. It will also strengthen men's willpower to stay true north on the straight and narrow path to salvation as a worthy disciple among God's chosen people.

Dear Lord, save us all!

Notes:

_____

_____

_____

_____

_____

_____

_____

_____

_____

_____

_____

_____

Epilogue

Whether biological or spiritual in nature, for a man, there is no better achievement in life than to be a successful father. There is no better reward in life than to see your faith-filled family living a peaceful life, nourished by God's grace. But the masculine journey can be difficult. The world is scheming constantly to separate fathers from the one true God and Loving Father, and to fracture the foundation of faith that leads men and their families to true happiness.

Tools for the journey are many – and a father's tool chest is his heart. When a father's heart embraces God, the tool chest grows and overflows through grace, offering virtues that extend into and enliven the hearts of the family that the father leads to God. Much wisdom is gained by the intentional father who composes himself through humility and selflessness and who uses his trials and failures as opportunities to grow. This wisdom instills within him a moral compass that guides all his decision-making and begins to work unconsciously within the hearts of the family he nurtures. As he lovingly answers his call to action, and as he roots his character in fair and honorable decision-making, he begins to change the world around him. His efforts to hand on the faith-filled gifts of the New Covenant and the sacraments now form his family's foundation of faith, which cascades to the generations to come.

As fathers, we must understand and accept that every decision and position we take, through our words and actions, affect our families. If we become complacent to what society dictates as acceptable, then we separate our families from our foundation of faith. If we fail to challenge false truths, perceived as reality for those living in and of this world, and we fail to protect our families from the many worldly causes that try to capture their hearts, then they will lose their way as they face the world on their own.

Humility and composure are our go-to tools that must be sharpened constantly to reflect and instill virtue within the families we nurture. By taking our God-given place within our families, we become the loving authority that our families count on and turn to for direction. This contradicts what society dictates, where the father figure is devalued and diminished. By always putting our families first and by our selfless actions, we pull our families above this worldly view, and we rest in the truth seen through God's grace as we love our families as Christ loves His Church.

There is no mistake in the repetitive nature of the terms used within the chapters of this book – terms such as *competency*, *intent*, and *foundation of faith*. Repetition is a tool that helps us learn. I challenge all fathers who have grown families to share their tools of experience and wisdom, gained through trials and failures, with young fathers. Help them understand the value of our foundation of faith; how it cascades throughout life; how true peace of heart and mind in this world comes only through the intentional application of these truths and faith-filled gifts within the families they nurture.

A prayer to strengthen my family's faith is what guided me in sharing this journey with you. At first, my prayer stopped at that, my family. A moment of grace, however, revealed to me that God's intent within my prayer, was to reach into and strengthen His entire faith-filled family. I felt an undeniable call to action to reach into the hearts of fathers building a foundation of faith within the families they nurture. I hope that the life lessons and competencies shared within this book will lead other fathers to a clearer understanding of their rightful place within their families and at the table of God.

Before we can lead, we must first follow…

A Final Call to Action...
"What is Truth?"

What is truth, and how can we discern and identify real truth from all the confusion wrought by the many versions of truth, or situational truths, that are now presented to us as real truth?

In the process of seeking out and discerning real truth, we must first accept, understand, and make ourselves aware to the fact that truth is first revealed to us by an authority.

So, how is truth revealed, and by what authority? In the world, truth is revealed to us through the New Covenant teachings of Jesus Christ. In society, mankind gives authority to our elected officials to govern. With the origins of the way truth is determined and revealed, now understood, can we see the importance of the truth that has been revealed to the world through the authority of Jesus Christ to be held in the hearts and minds of our elected officials? One would have hoped that the actions of these men and women, whom we gave the authority to govern and write laws, would have reflected and revealed "real truth" within our society.

An unbiased objective look reveals that we have brought ourselves to an interpretation and perception of truth that is lacking good will or intention. The impression of truth reflected in society no longer mirrors or even bears a close resemblance to the guiding truth that our Creator, the author of all authority, revealed to the world. Somehow, over the generations, in our arrogance and pride, we came to believe that we are smarter and more evolved than previous generations. We think that we need not submit our free will to any authority. We lost sight of the humility needed to see and accept the fullness of truth revealed to us by God's authority, which is imperative to peacefully govern in the world.

Over the generations, our civil authorities denounced the divine origins of truth and imposed their own personal will or "situational truths" upon those they govern. This form of governing created divisions within society, and suppressed the virtues of humility, honor, and integrity within our societal posture. Many of our civil authorities, elected and appointed, act more like unfavorable kings over their subjects than guardians of the common good. Unwittingly emptied of good intent, to many, this seems to be accepted behavior in the court of public opinion. I have no doubt that many of our civil authorities are unaware they are denying real truth, as they forcefully enact their situational truths upon us. Society stepped so far away from God's law over the generations that now, deep within their will, they believe what they are perpetuating to be real truth. Subsequently, real truth has fallen victim to the politician's clouded, socially accepted situational truths. Understanding the origins and authority of real truth comes through humility and wisdom reflected in love of neighbor, which at the moment is rarely seen in our society.

Knowing and recognizing the difference between real truth and situational truth will be an important first step in our journey back to God's law. Moral posture and family values, grounded in real truth, needs to be restored to bring peaceful order back to our homes and communities. There is great meaning to why we place our hand on a Bible, in a court of law, when we are asked to swear to tell the truth, the whole truth, and nothing but the truth, so help me God...

This knowledge shared goes out as a call to action to all intentional men and fathers. Take your rightful place in society and fight the good fight toward taking back our families and communities.

Our understanding of truth is not so different from what Pontius Pilate faced nearly 2,000 years ago when he asked Jesus, "What is truth?" (John 18:38). Jesus is Truth! The very Word of God might stand directly before us, meek and without malice. Ever doubtful and distant from truth, we turn away, just as Pilate did. We fail to trust the reality of what we see and hear. We concede to the cultivated cultural, political, and extreme religious factions that crowd around us, competing for our attention, demanding our submission.

God understands that the world needs authority figures to help communities prosper and ultimately to lead people of good will back to Him (Luke 9:1-6). This is as true for the heads of households as it is for the heads of state. We face a relentless, uphill battle; but be not afraid, for with God, all things are possible (Matt 19:26)!

Prayer to St. Joseph, the Foster Father of Jesus Christ and Patron Saint in the New Covenant of the Universal Church

St. Joseph was the first father ever to be challenged with accepting and understanding the universal church (meaning the Body of Christ both in heaven and on earth). He did this without any knowledge of what the New Covenant was to reveal. In the face of adversity, St. Joseph selflessly composed himself in a spirit of humility. With unwavering faith, he answered his call to action within the Holy Family.

We can all grow in our understanding of the New Covenant by learning from the example of St. Joseph, who employed his free will by trusting and following the will of God. St. Joseph shows all fathers how to be selfless. Through his example, we can make the hard choices required to hand on all that is known and shared through the New Covenant and the sacraments as the foundation of faith. We are accountable to God to lead our families. If we do this well, with intent and perseverance, like St. Joseph, then we can take our rightful place at the table of God as good and worthy servants.

This prayer to St. Joseph can help all spiritual and biological fathers, through the inevitable adversity they will face, as they work to preserve the sanctity of the family.

Prayer to Saint Joseph, Patron of the Universal Church[9]

O Glorious Saint Joseph, Patron of the Universal Church, I implore thee to obtain from the Hearts of Jesus and Mary, the preservation of our remnant Catholic Community and all its members, from all division, dissension, and discord.

Do thou, faithful Guardian of the Holy Family, grant that our spiritual family, all the members of our remnant Catholic Community, shall ever be united in the Bonds of Faith and Charity, and shall remain always of One Heart, Mind and Soul in the Hearts of Jesus and Mary.

Saint Joseph, special Protector of our Community, do thou guide, bless, and protect us against the attacks, of all our enemies and detractors. Through Our Lord Jesus Christ, Who lives and reigns with the Father and the Holy Spirit, One God, forever, unto ages of ages. Amen.

Let's re-read and focus on one line from the prayer: "from all division, dissension, and discord." If you believe in Jesus Christ, you are my brother in the Universal Church, and nothing divides us from this truth. No one who believes in Jesus Christ is excluded. Wherever we are, on our spiritual paths, and in the arch of life, we are all called to treat each other with unconditional love and respect. We are all God's children, diverse and unique in our own ways, but sharing a common journey toward our eternal home and a seat at our Father's table. Faith always leads to love.

St. Joseph, pray for us.

About the Author

Ray Haywood is a devoted husband to his wife, Natalie. They have been married for the past 30 years. Together they intentionally raised two faith-filled sons, Nicholas and Frank, within the foundation of faith, the sacraments. Ray shares in more than 26 years of willful fatherhood and parenting experience. Now living in North Carolina, Ray and Natalie operate a small family-owned car dealership. They are faithful parishioners of Saint Thomas Aquinas Catholic Church, in Charlotte, North Carolina. Through active parish involvement, Ray's family's faith continues to grow in the New Covenant teachings of the Catholic Church. He is devoted to handing on the faith-filled gifts to all men of good faith wherever they may be in their faith journey. He finds this to be his call to action in his own faith journey.

Footnotes

[1] Eldredge, John. Fathered by God: Learning What Your Dad Could Never Teach You. Nashville: Thomas Nelson, 2009. Print.

[2] Lewis, C. S. A Mind Awake: An Anthology of C. S. Lewis, Boston: Houghton Mifflin Harcourt, 2004. Print. p.168

[3] Lewis, C. S. The Screwtape Letters: With Screwtape Proposes a Toast. San Francisco: HarperCollins, 2001. Print. p. 28

[4] "Key Facts About Family Structure," Child Trends Databank. August 23, 2016. <https://www.childtrends.org/>

[5] Macmillan English Dictionary for Advanced Learners, 2 Ed. Edited by Michael Rundell. London: Macmillan ELT. 2007. Print.

[6] "Definition for Rote," Merriam-Webster Dictionary, accessed November 13, 2018. https://www.merriam-webster.com/

[7] Adams, Linda. "Learning a New Skill Is Easier Said than Done." Gordon Training International. n.d. http://www.gordontraining.com/

[8] "Humility," Catholic Answers, Catholic.com, accessed November 13, 2018. https://www.catholic.com/encyclopedia/humility

[9] Prayer to Saint Joseph, Patron of the Universal Church." CatholicTruth.net, accessed November 13, 2018 http://catholictruth.net/CTNet_RC/en/archive.asp?d=20150315S

Notes:

CPSIA information can be obtained
at www.ICGtesting.com
Printed in the USA
LVHW011127180520
655783LV00006B/320

9 781733 595704